Wobbly Lines Art NZ

Thank you for purchasing my 2018 CHRISTMAS Book.

Your support means so much to me!

A little about me. My name is Lynette Hansen-McNamara, and I have happily re-discovered my love for drawing after a hiatus of many years - hence the name Wobbly Lines. I have 3 grown children, 3 grown grand-children, 2 small grandsons (with another on the way), and 3 small great-grandsons - this keeps me very busy! I'm an avid reader, colourer, crafter, crocheter, and I try to do an Act of Kindness every day.

My style is whimsical, with a little bit of weird, and a side dish of eclectic. I like to draw flowers, sugar skulls, faerie houses, alphabets, garden gnomes, Santas, snowmen ... and I'm discovering new things to draw every day.

Let your inner child loose and have fun with my whimsical art! Due to the nature of my hand-drawn art, there will be wobbly lines that are part of the charm of non-digital art. I have not used any digital enhancements at all. **Some of the pages in this book have TWO pocket-sized/Postcard sized pictures on each page**. If you want, after colouring, cut them out and send as a postcard. If you print them directly onto thickish card you can send them as they are. If you print onto thin card, or paper {as I do}, just mount them onto card with a stick glue and a brayer, or double-sided tape after you've finished colouring. Pop on a stamp and post! The pages with **FOUR** images per page are Card Toppers, cut them out when you've finished colouring, and mount them onto a folded A4 piece of card. Embellish with glitter, rhinestones, washi tape, rubber stamps etc.

I invite you to join and share your finished page in my Facebook Coloring Group at:
facebook.com/groups/WobblyLines
OR - my Art Page on Facebook:
facebook.com/WobblyLines

*The images remain the **copyrighted property of Lynette Hansen-McNamara of Wobbly Lines Art NZ**, and copies of the blank images may not be shared or uploaded to any social media site. You may not sell or share printed copies nor use the images for any commercial use without my written consent. Thank you for respecting my art.

I dedicate this book to my dear friend Shawn Bobar, for encouraging and supporting me. Without her this book would never have been made. Her contribution has been invaluable, she has my deepest gratitude.

~Lynette~

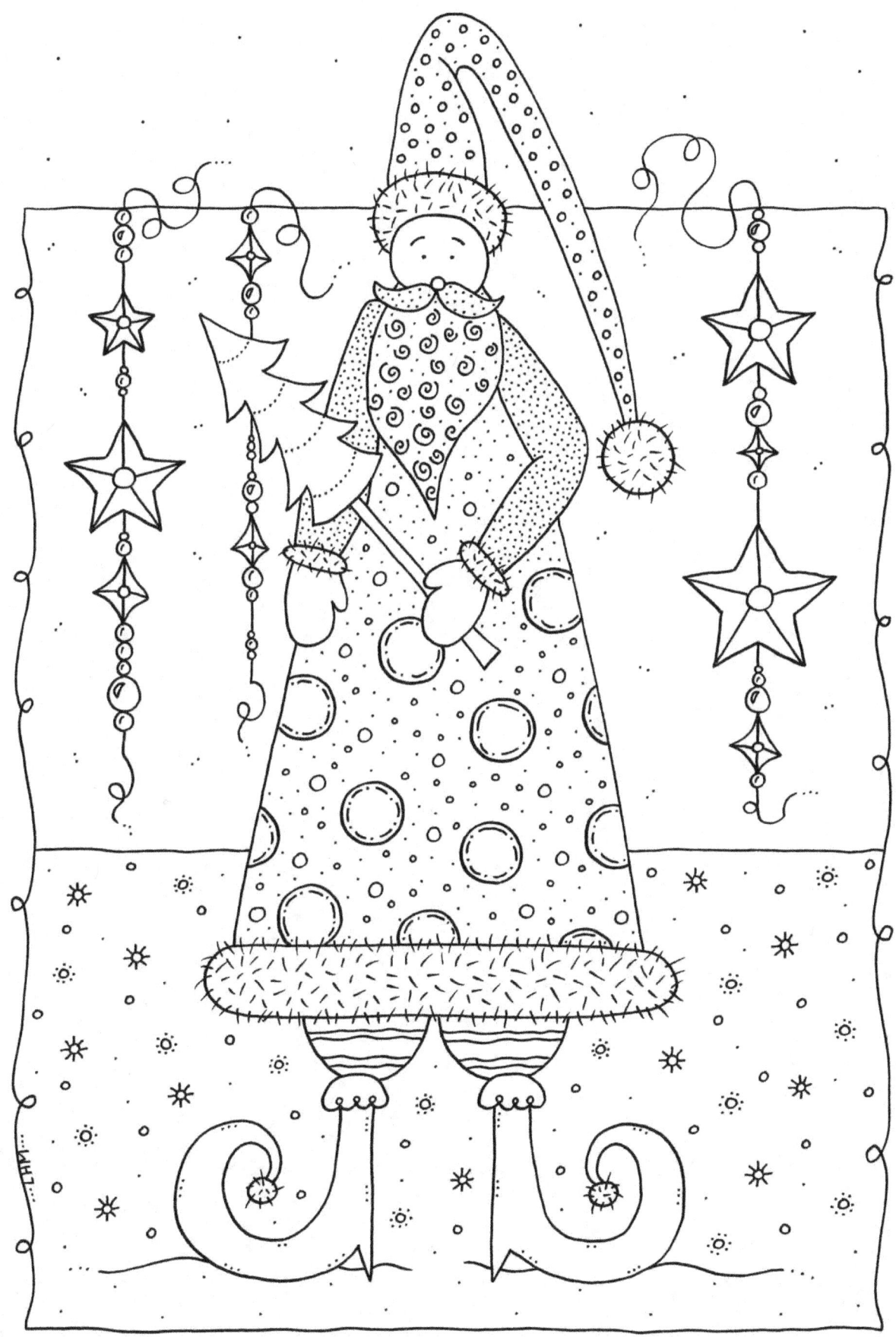

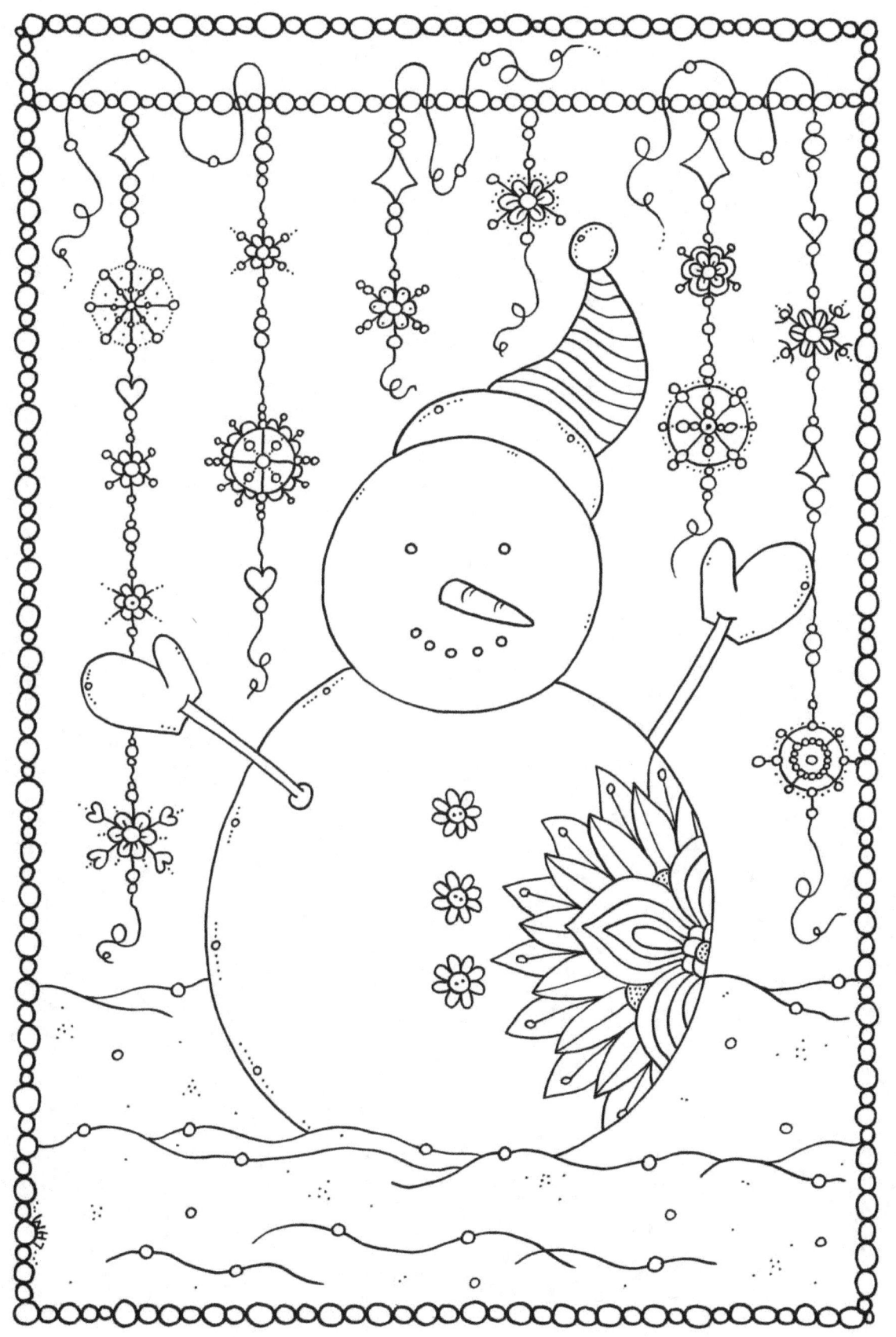

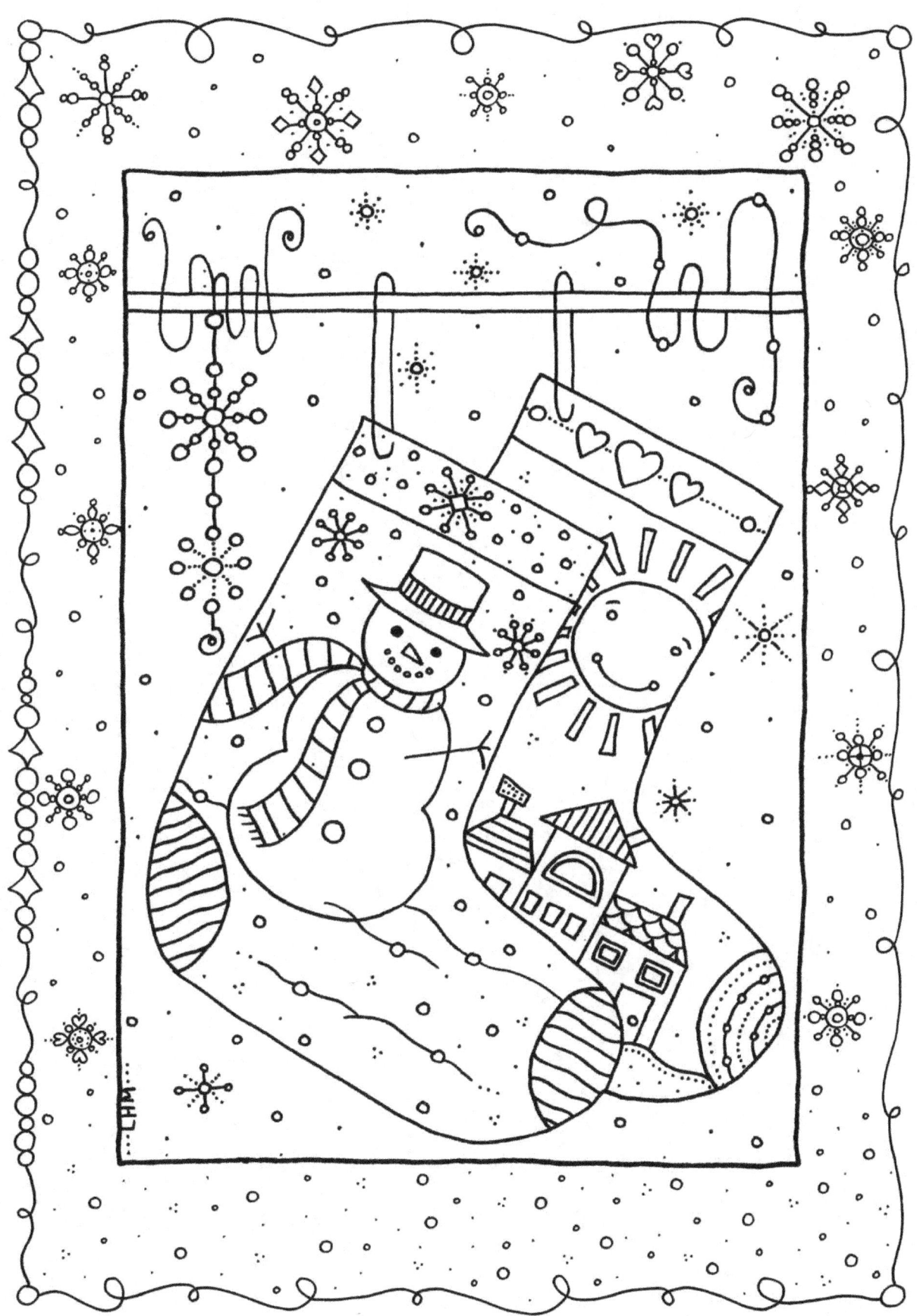

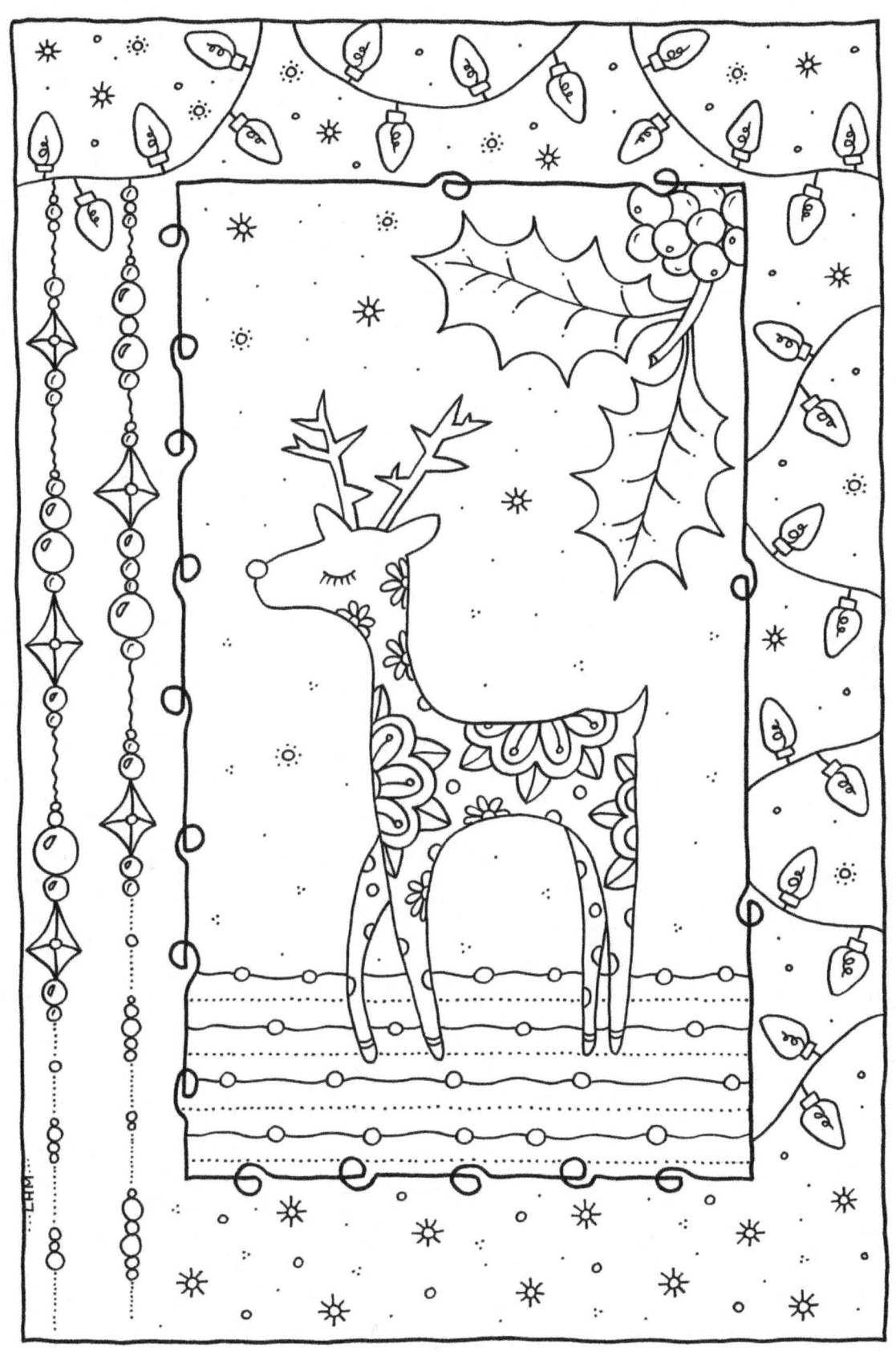

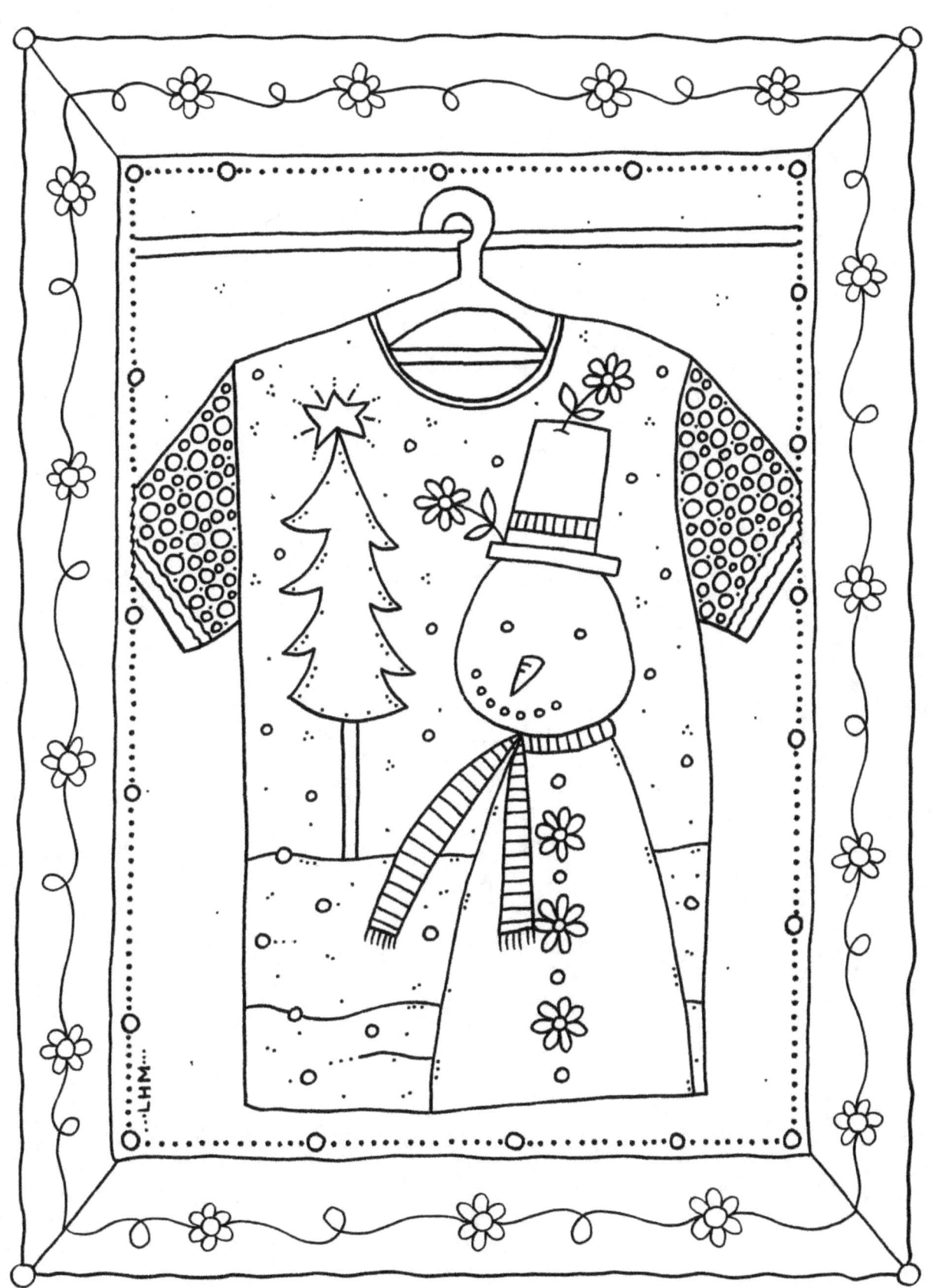

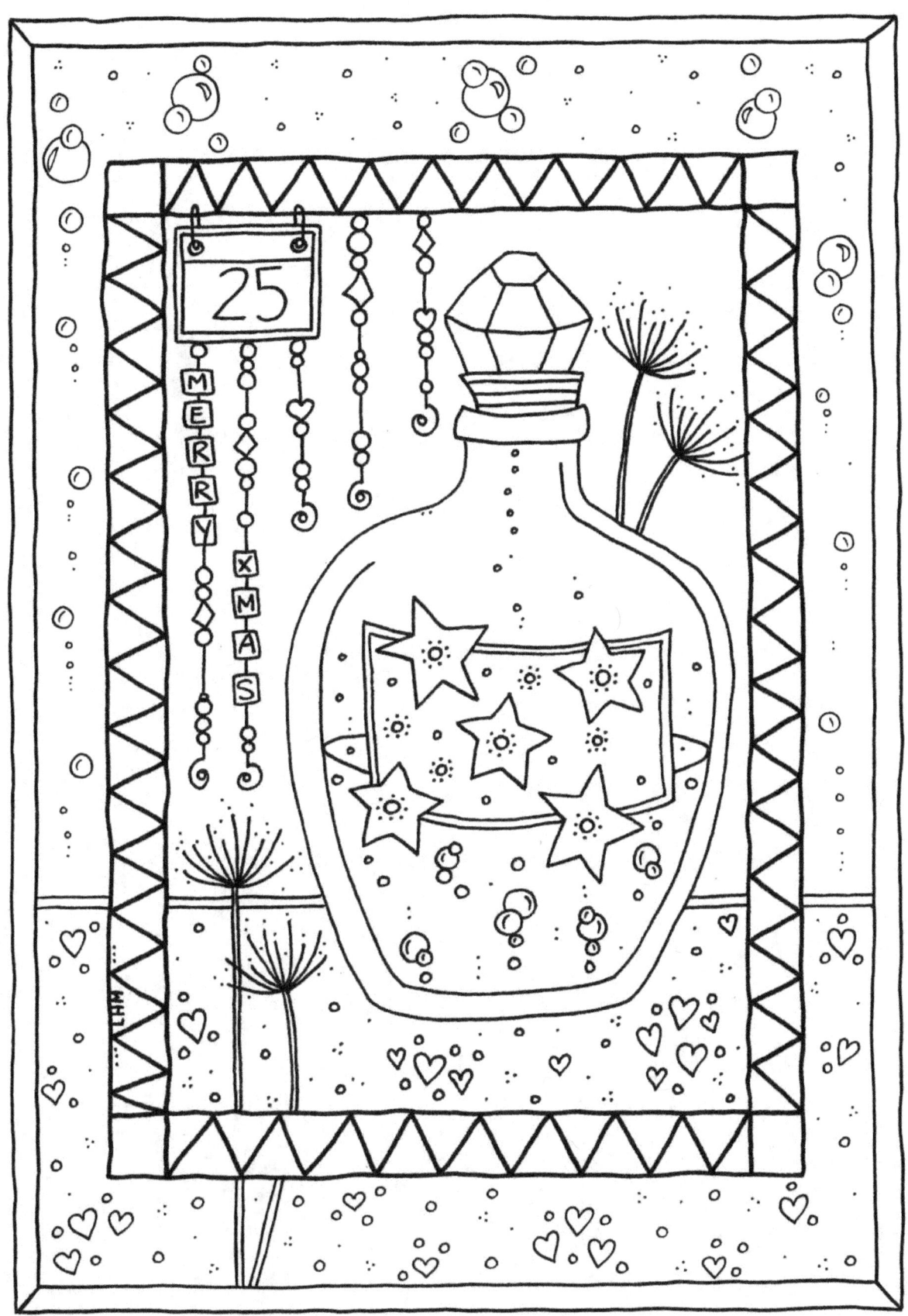

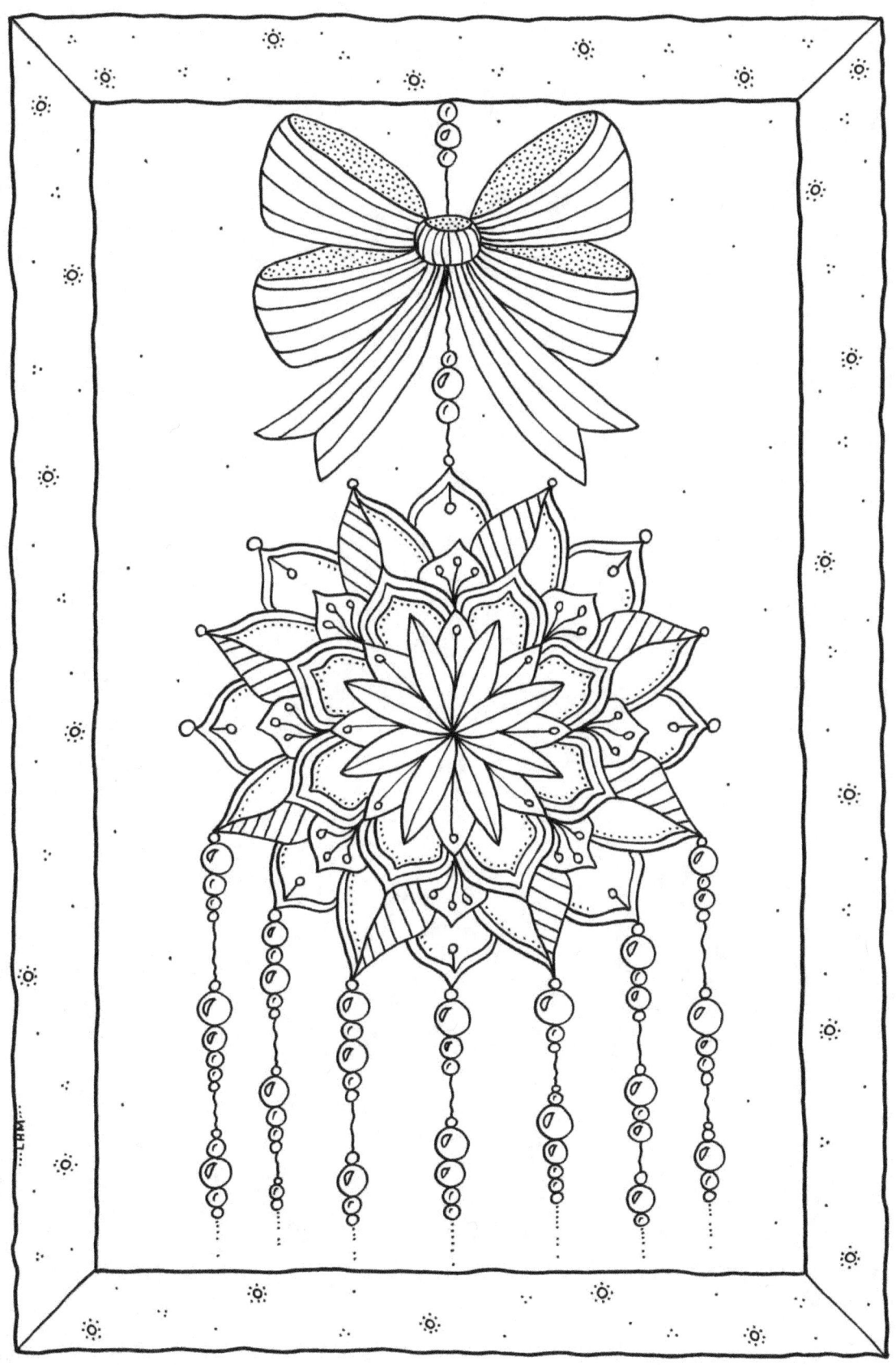

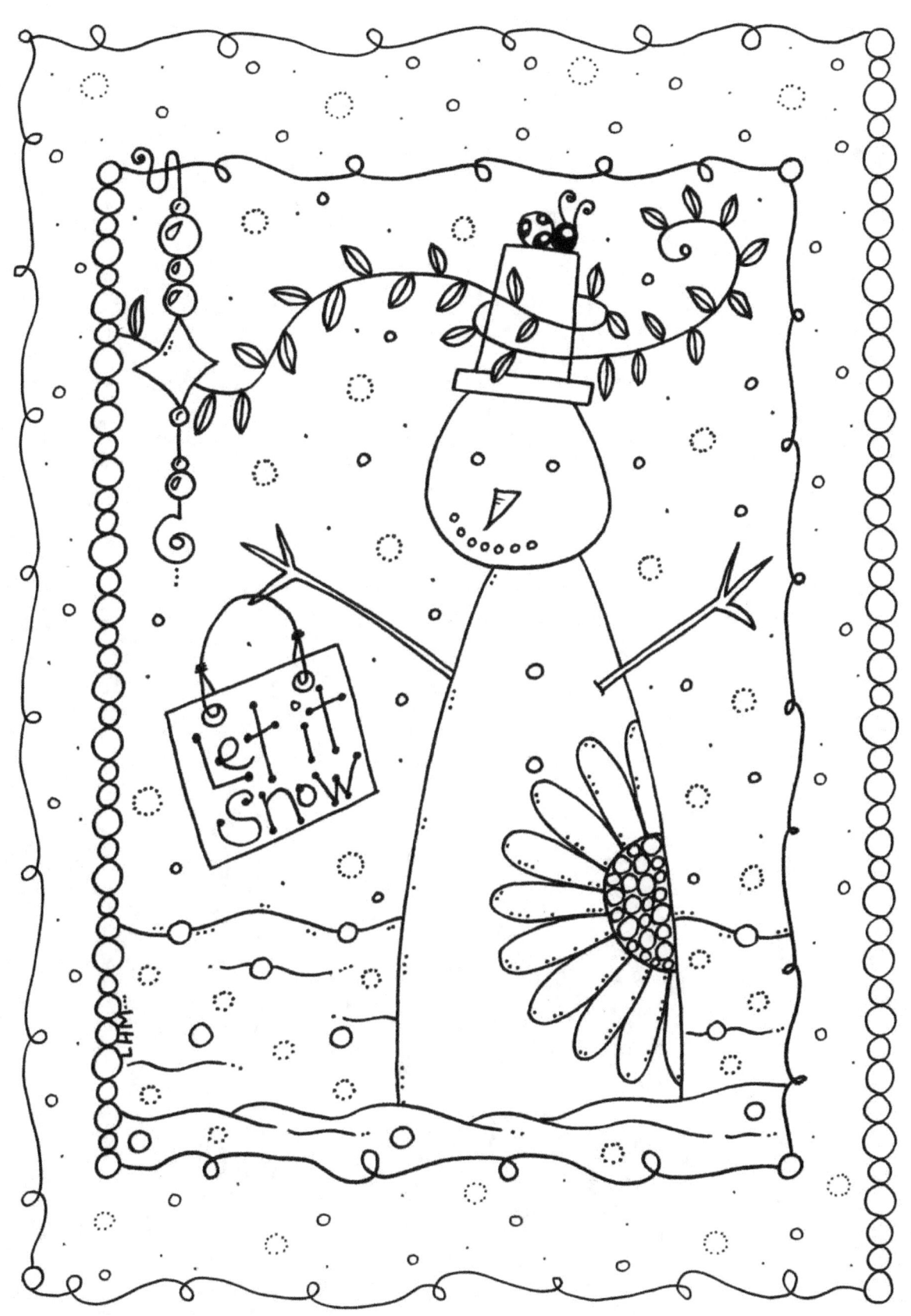

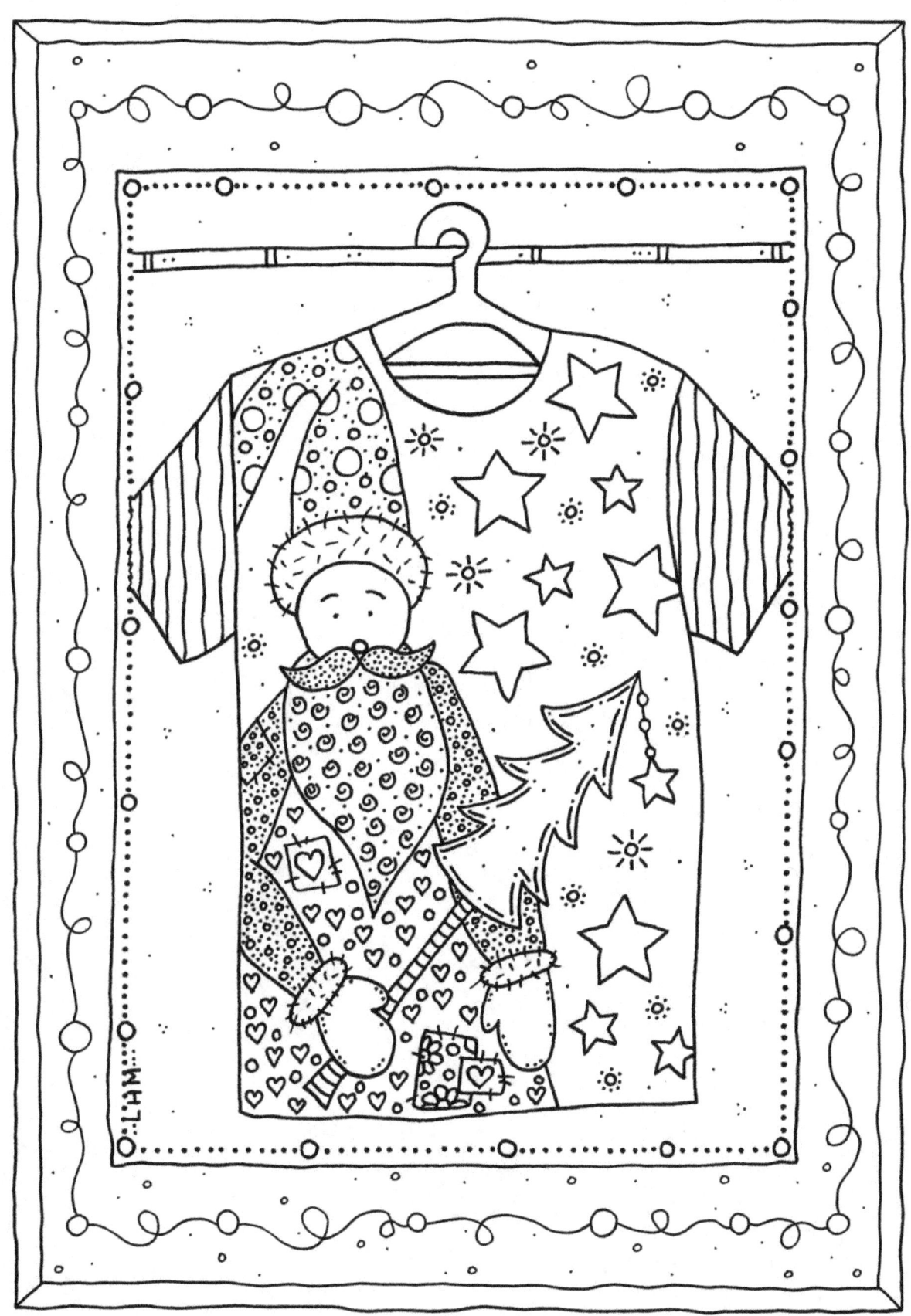

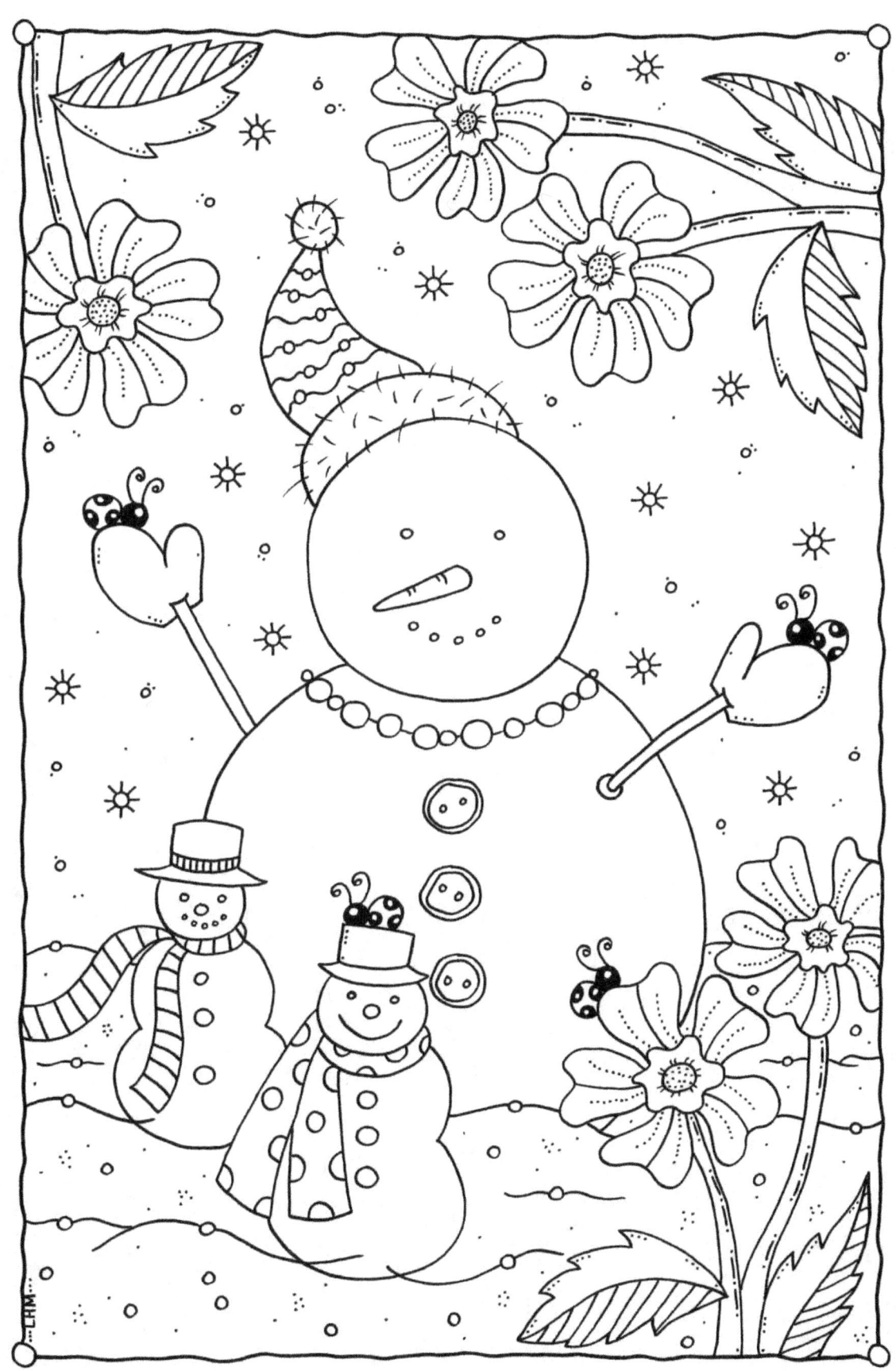

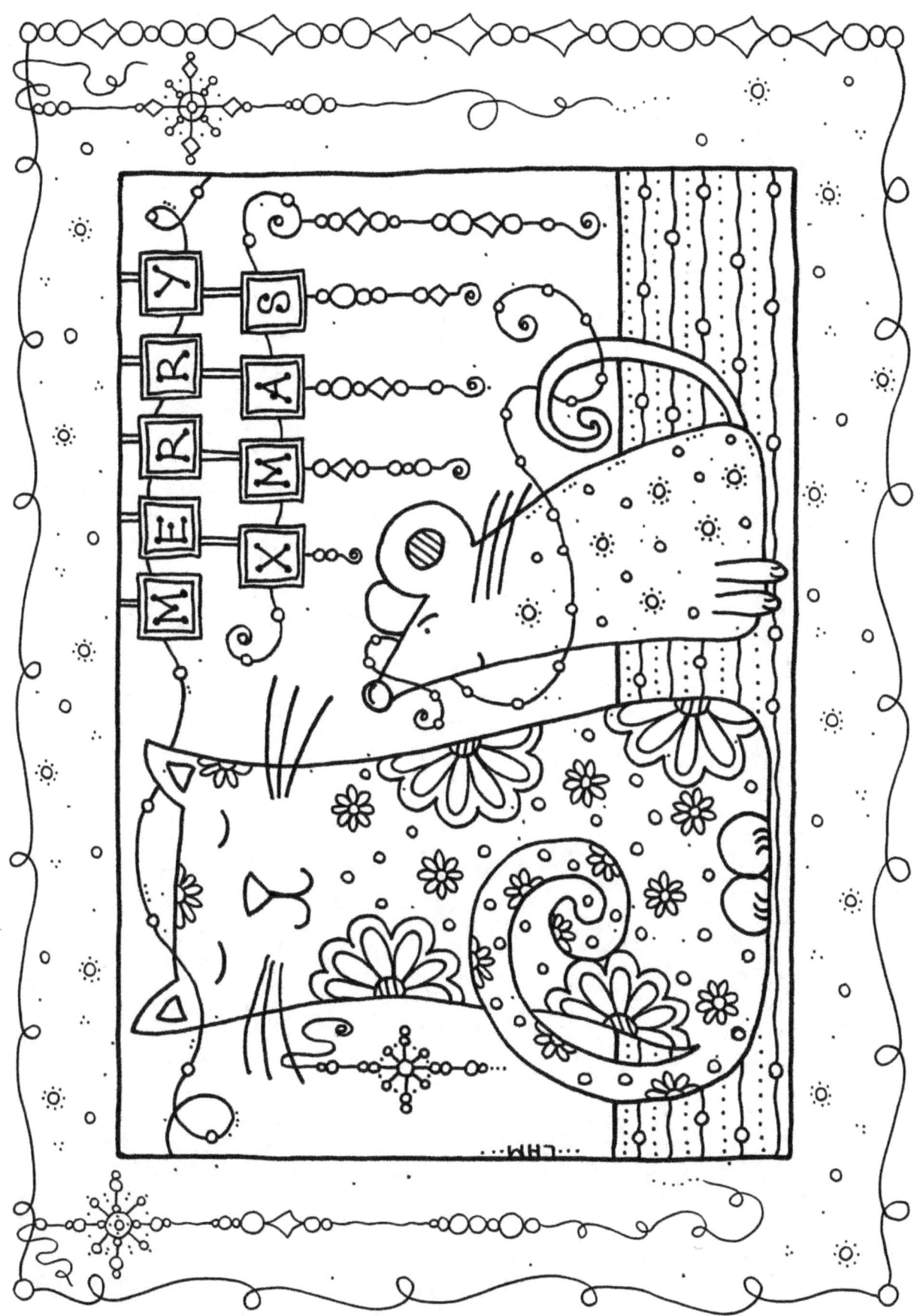

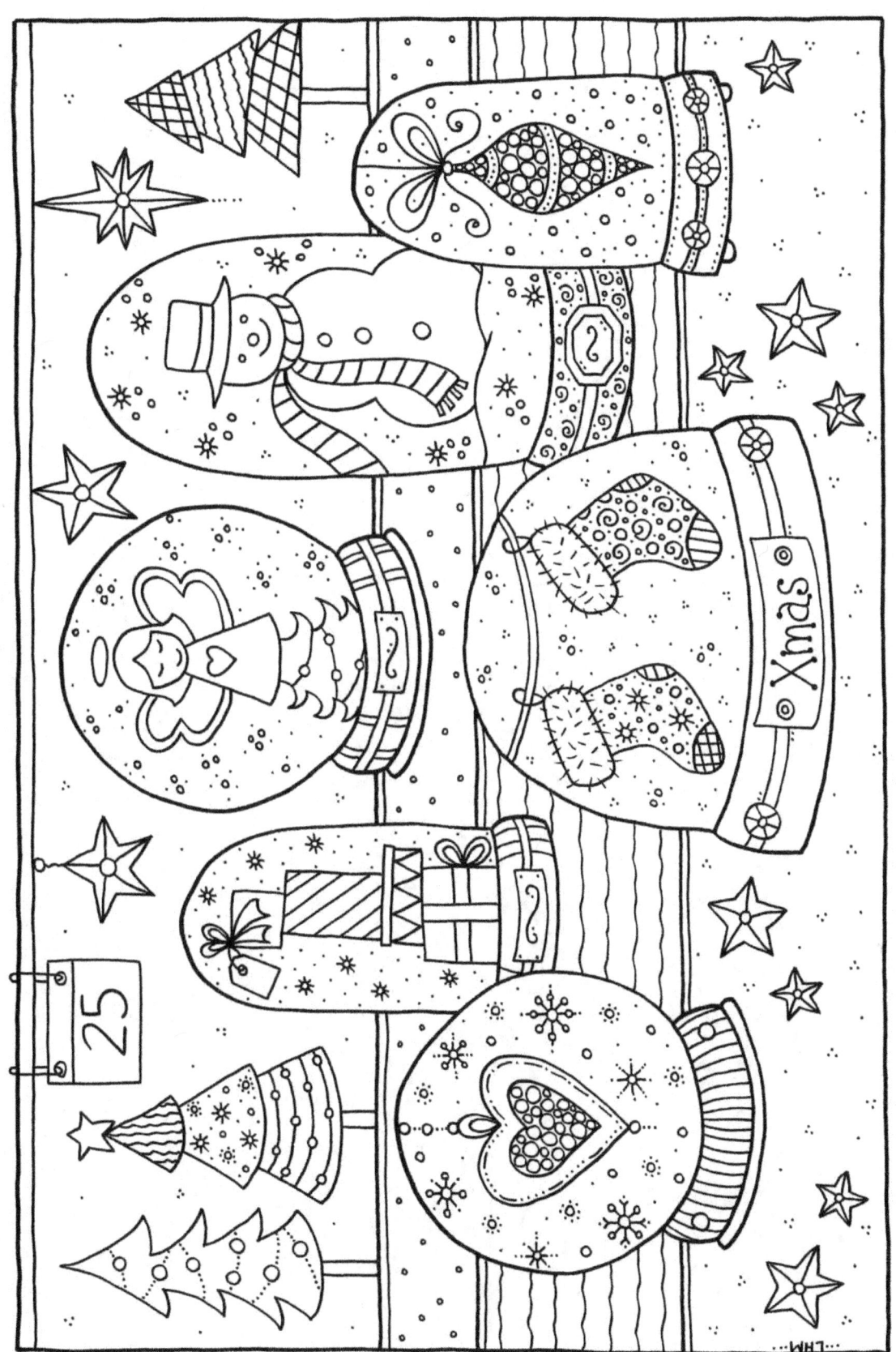

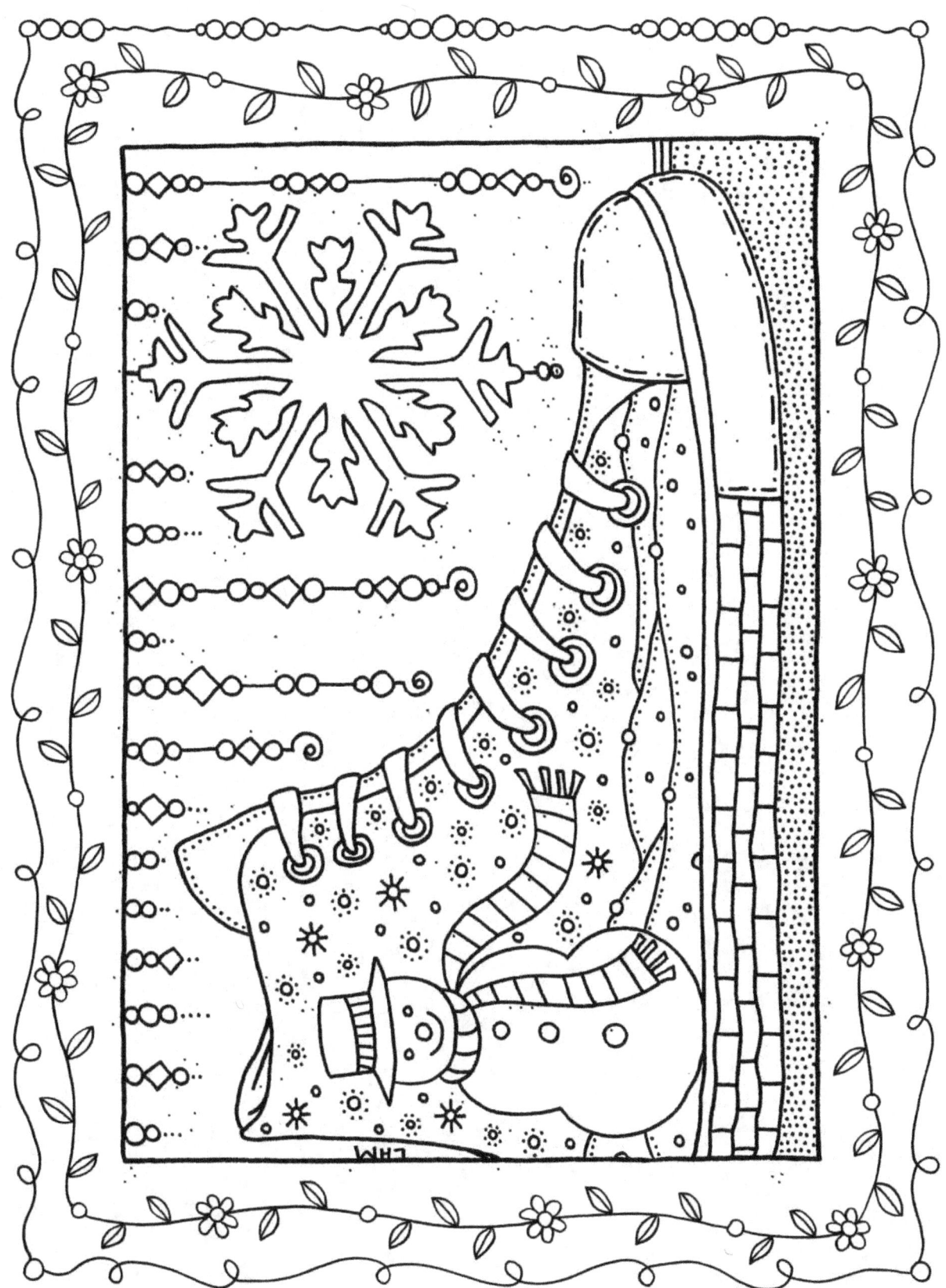

A5 - Postcard size images

The images in this section are all A5 - Postcard sized.

You have my permission to photocopy them for your own personal use. They may not be used for commercial use without my prior written consent.

If you would like to make these into postcards either use the original images from the book, or photocopy them first. After coloring, cut them out, and send them as a postcard, or large cards. If you print them directly onto thickish card you can send them as they are. If you print onto thin card, or paper (as I do), just mount them onto card with stick glue and a brayer, or double-sided tape after coloring.

You can then add embellishments. Glitter, washi tape, rubber stamping, 3D embellishments if you're feeling adventurous. Have fun, and experiment.

Then pop on a stamp and post!

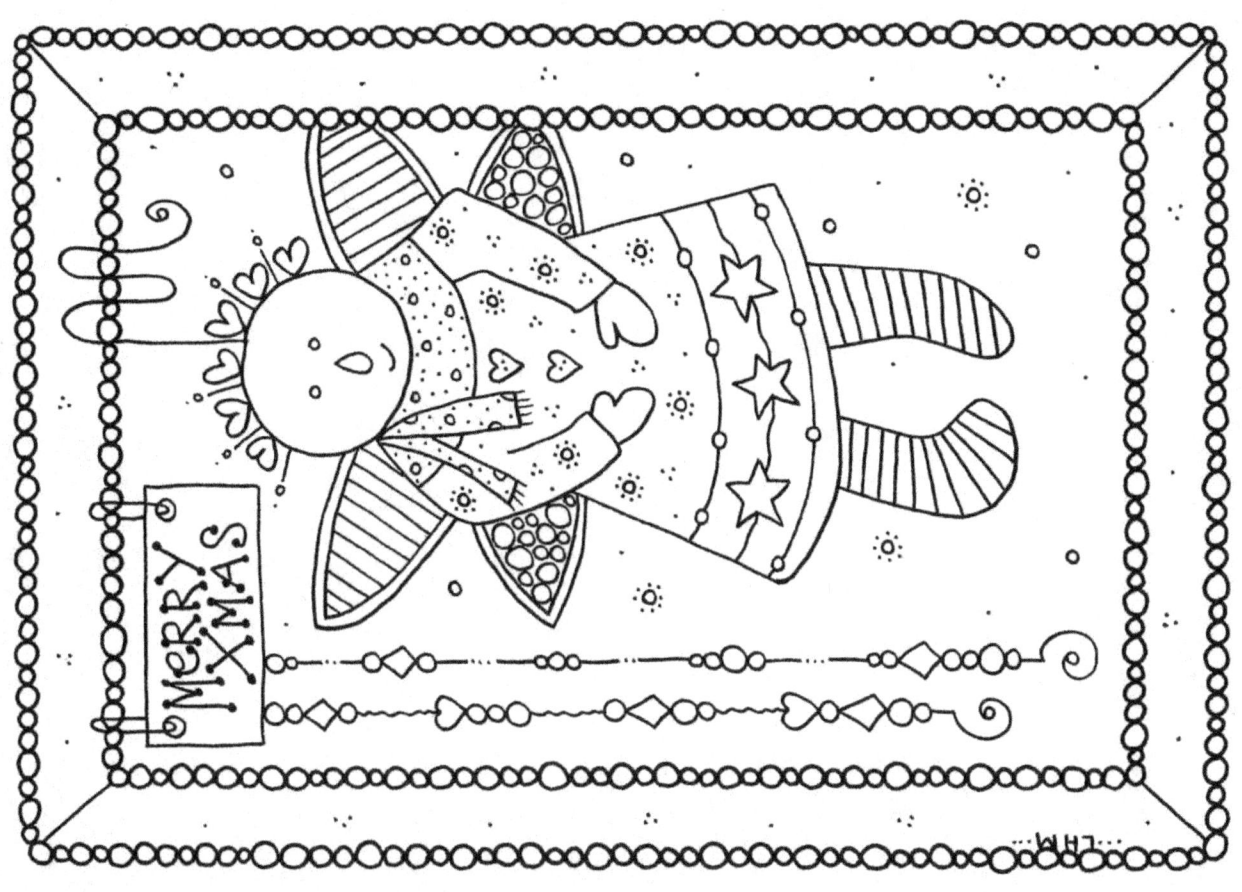
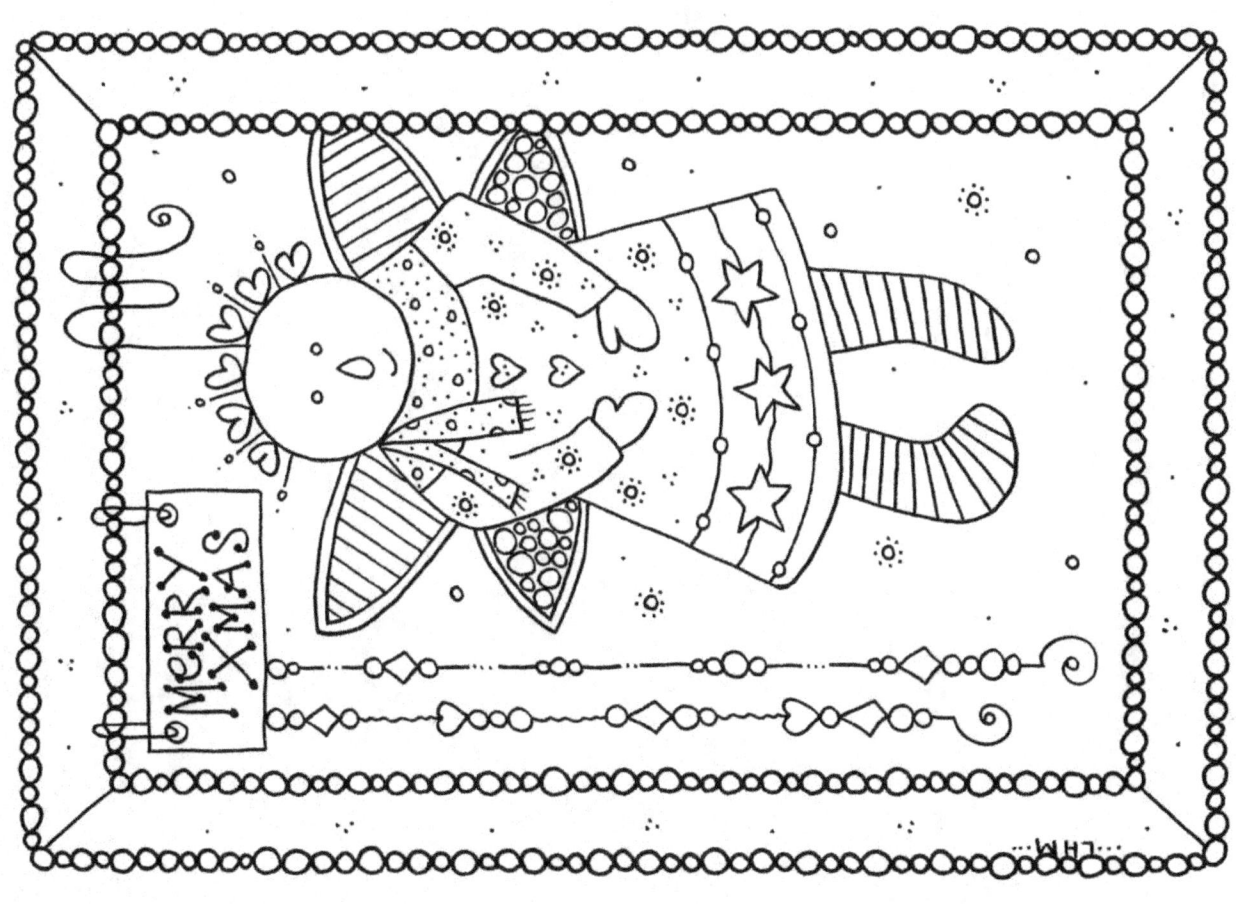

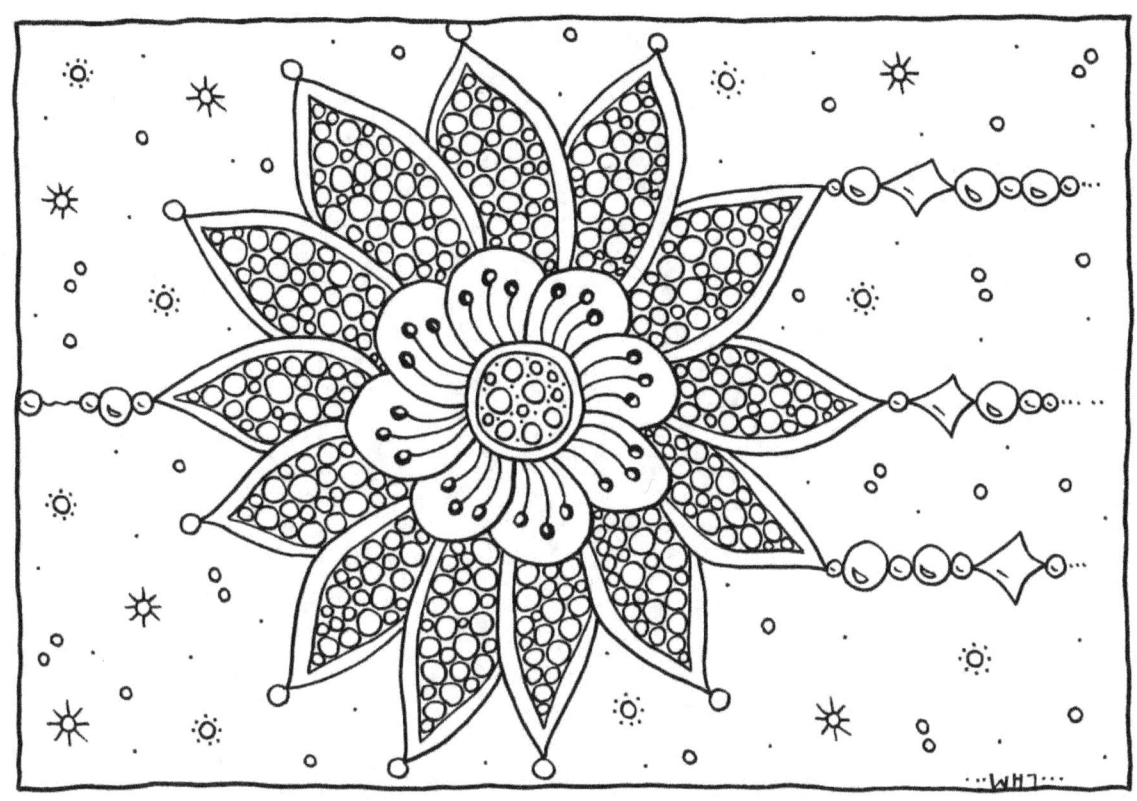
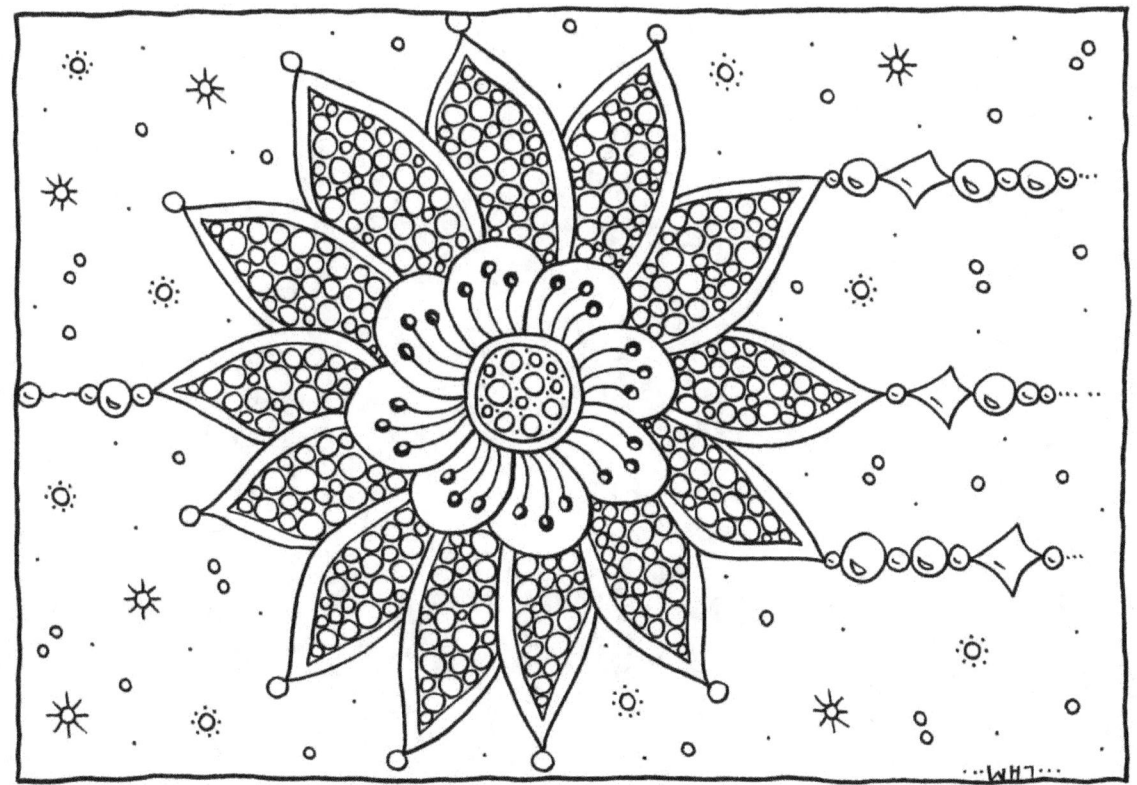

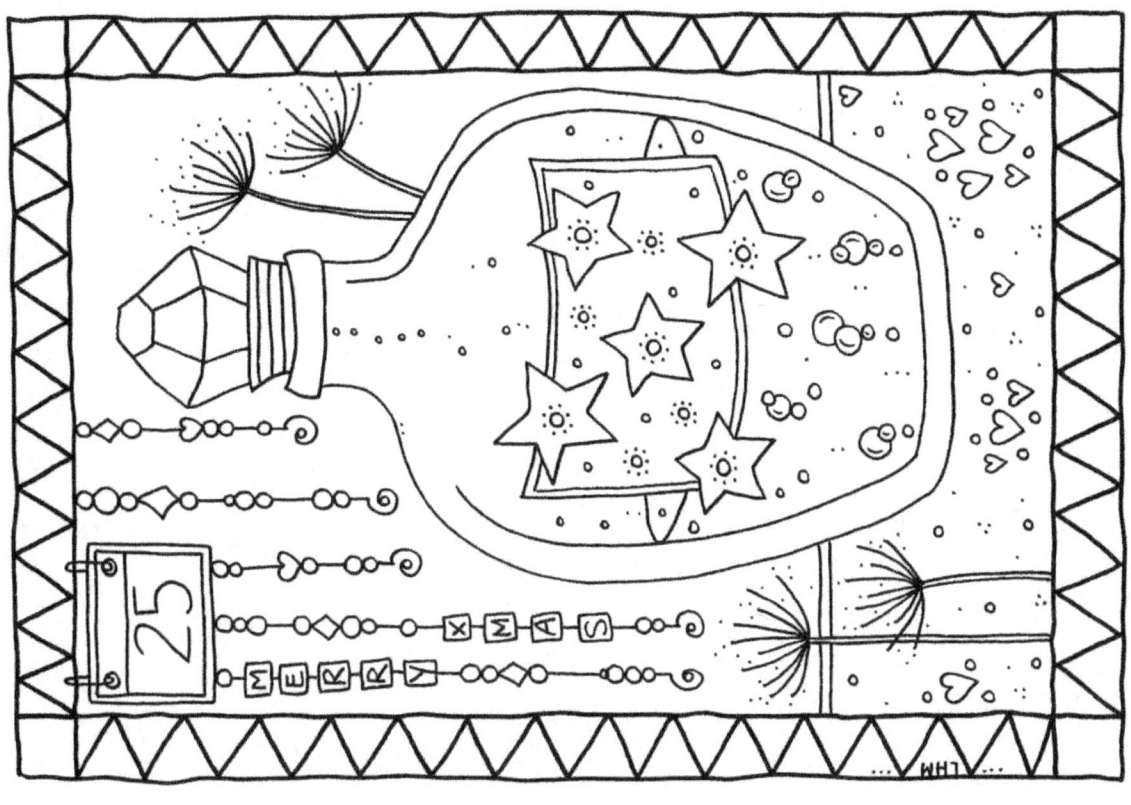
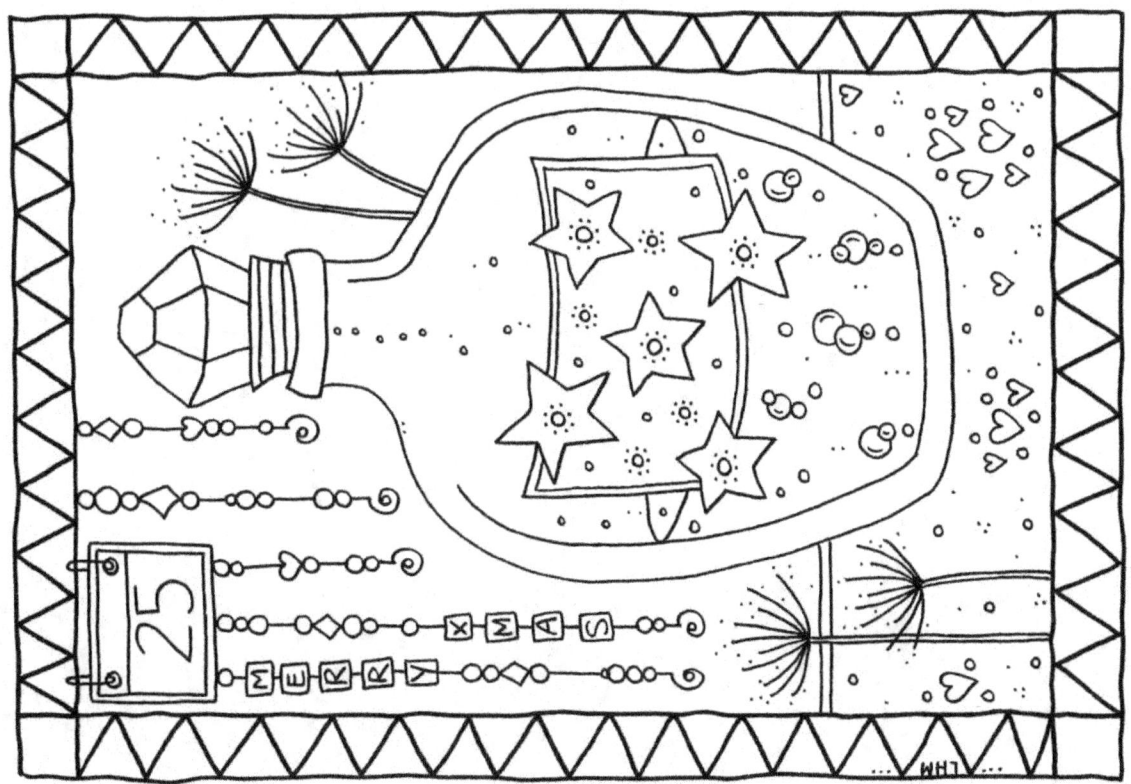

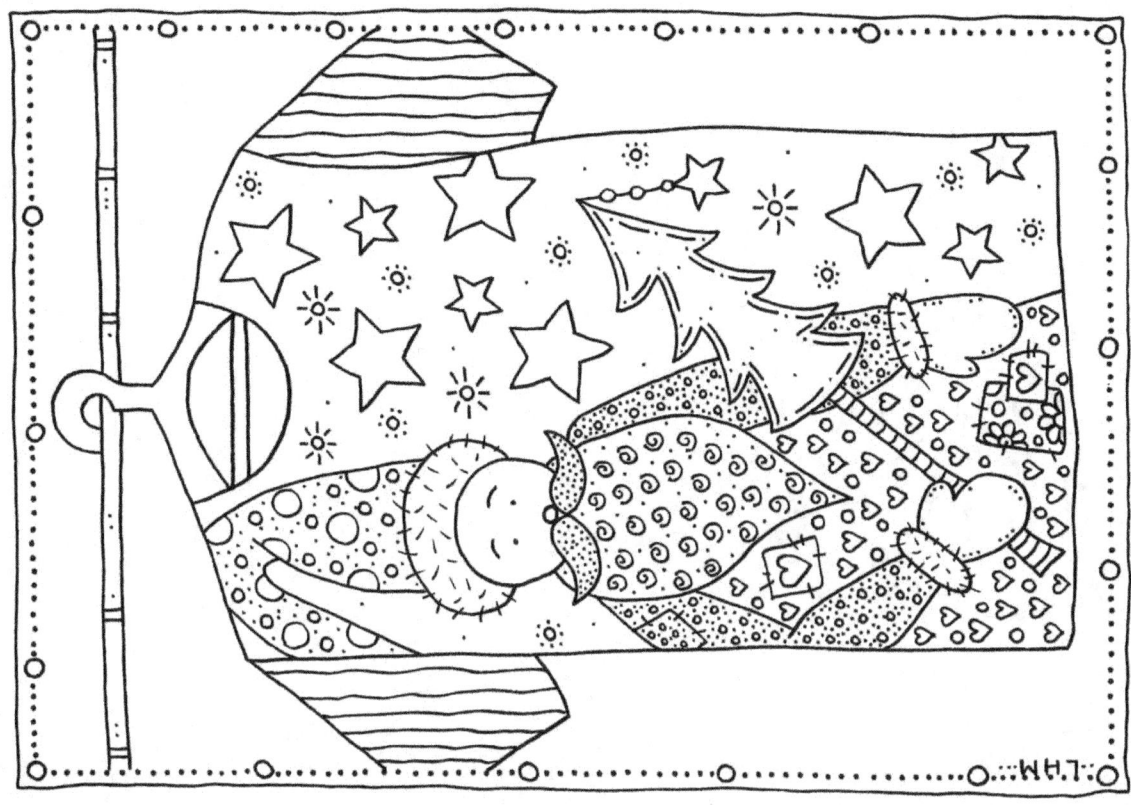
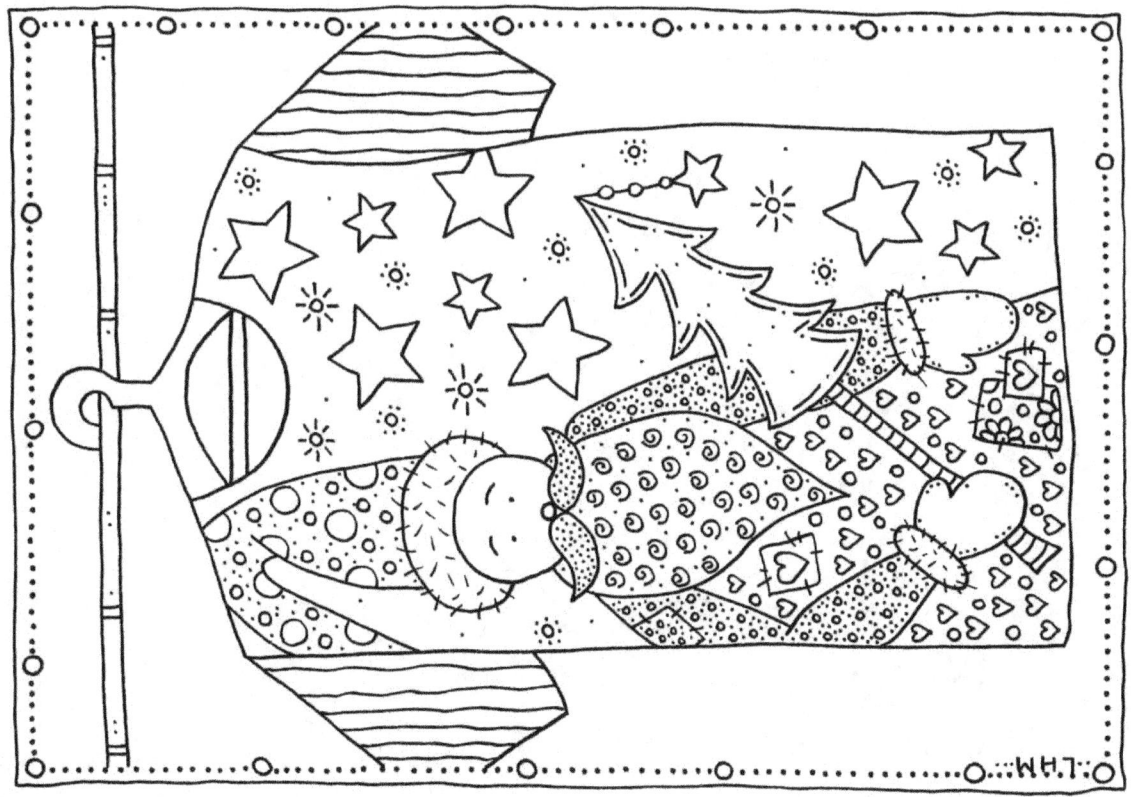

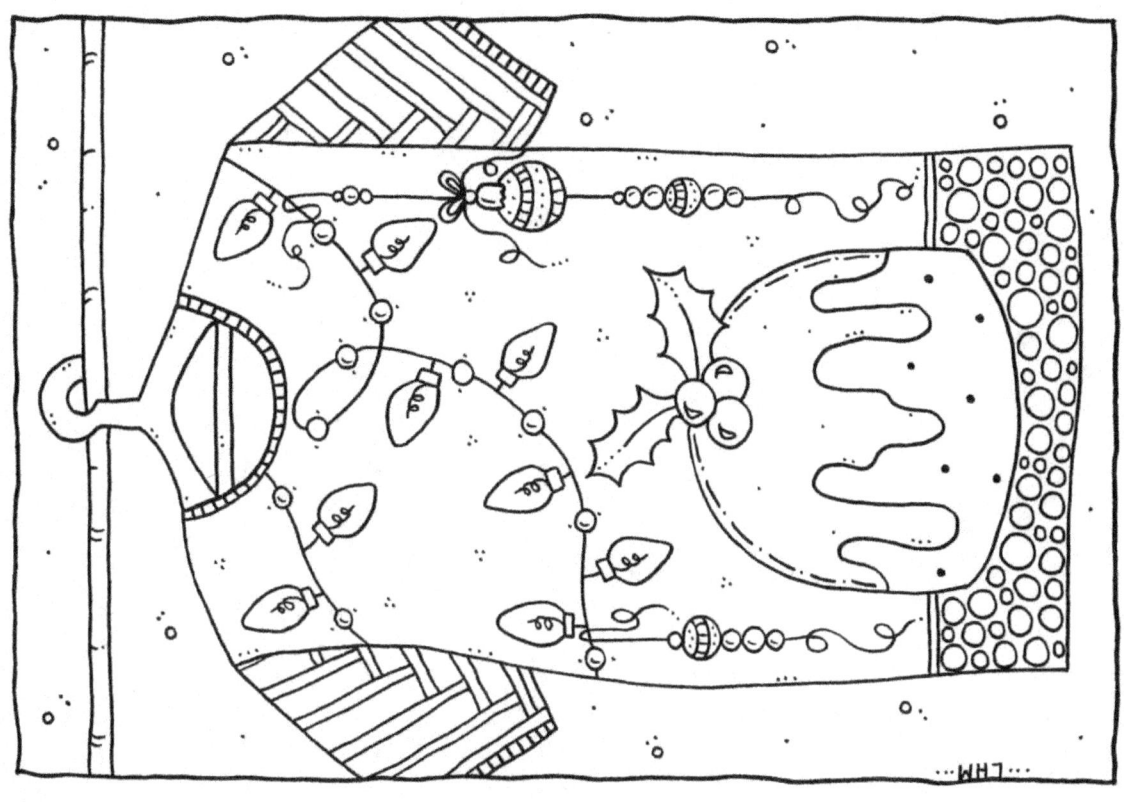
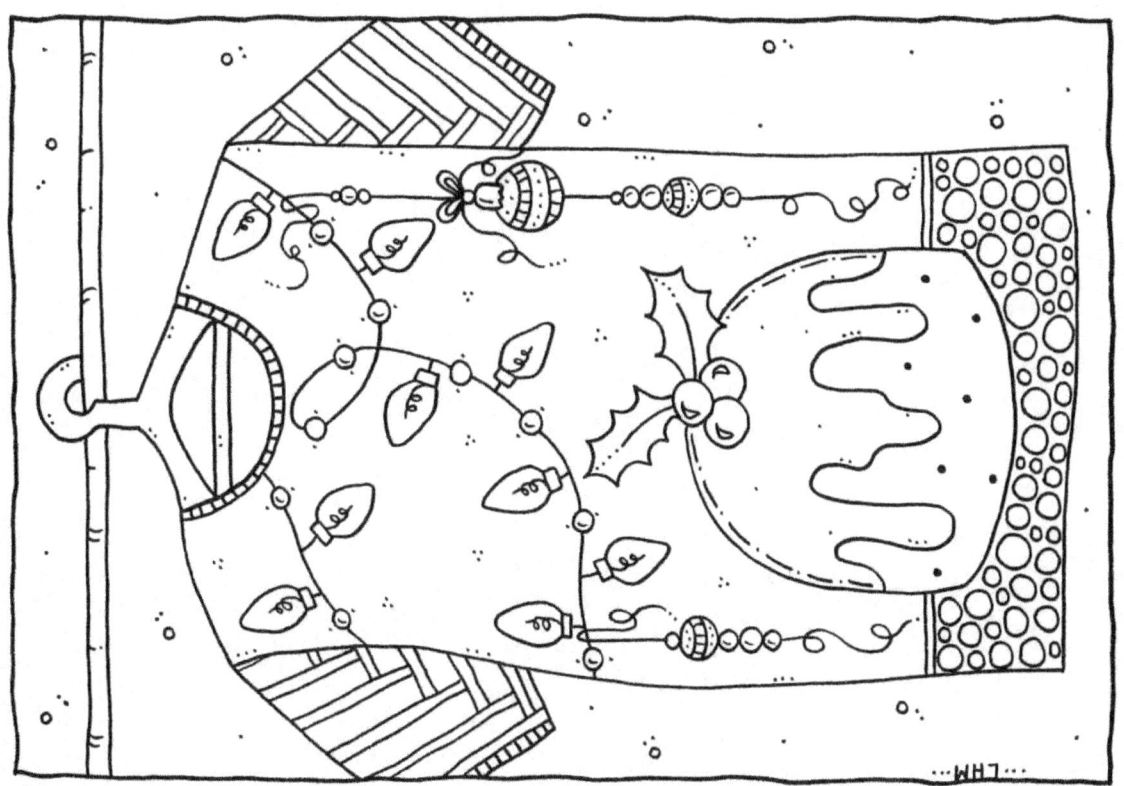

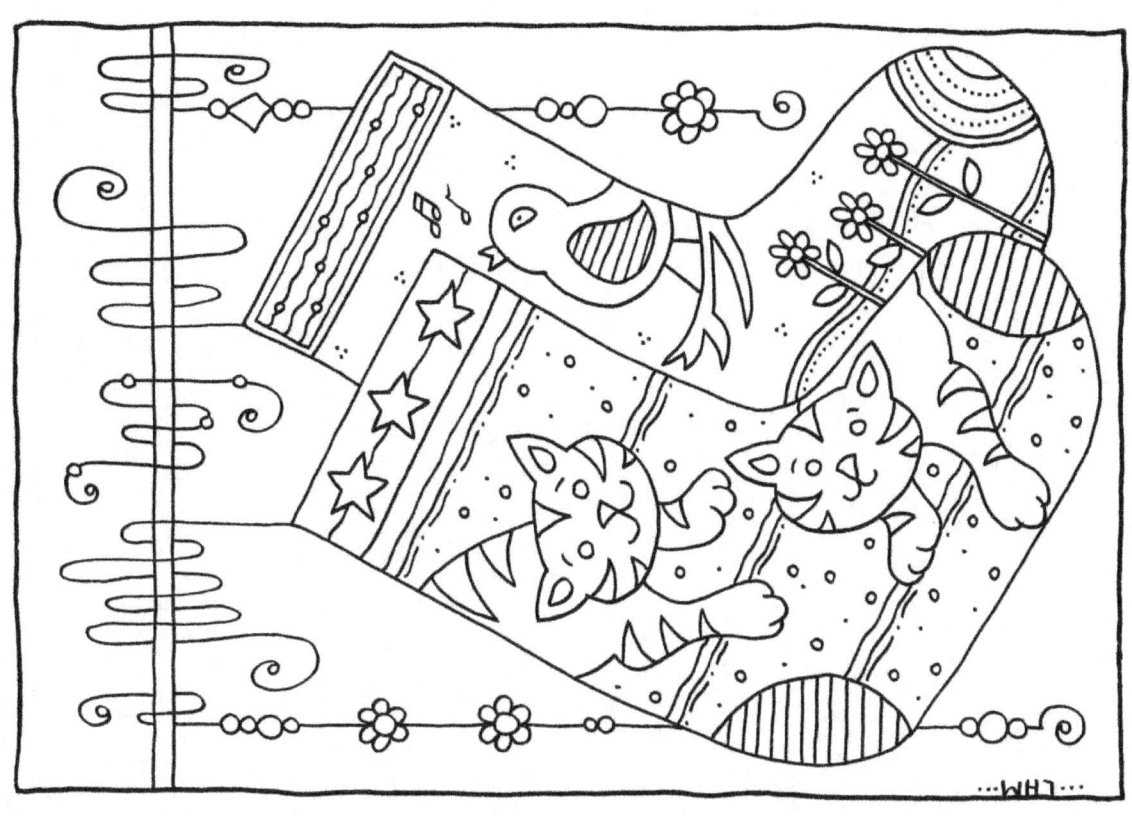
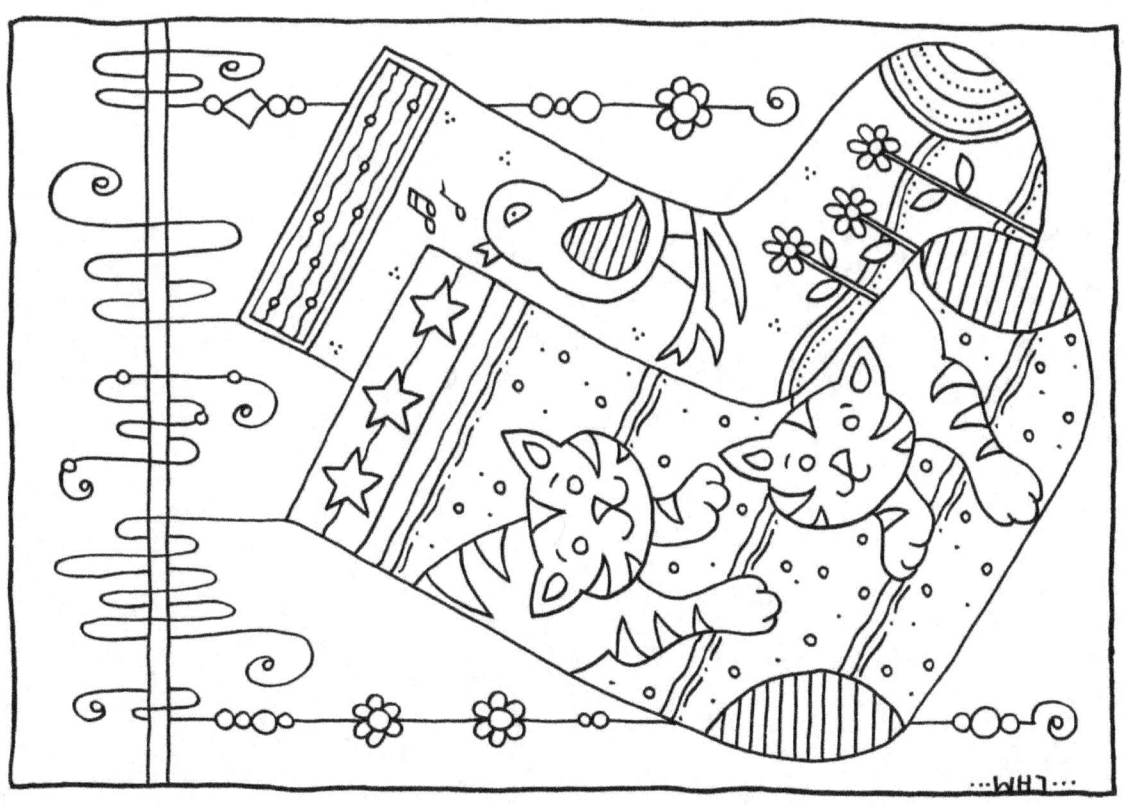

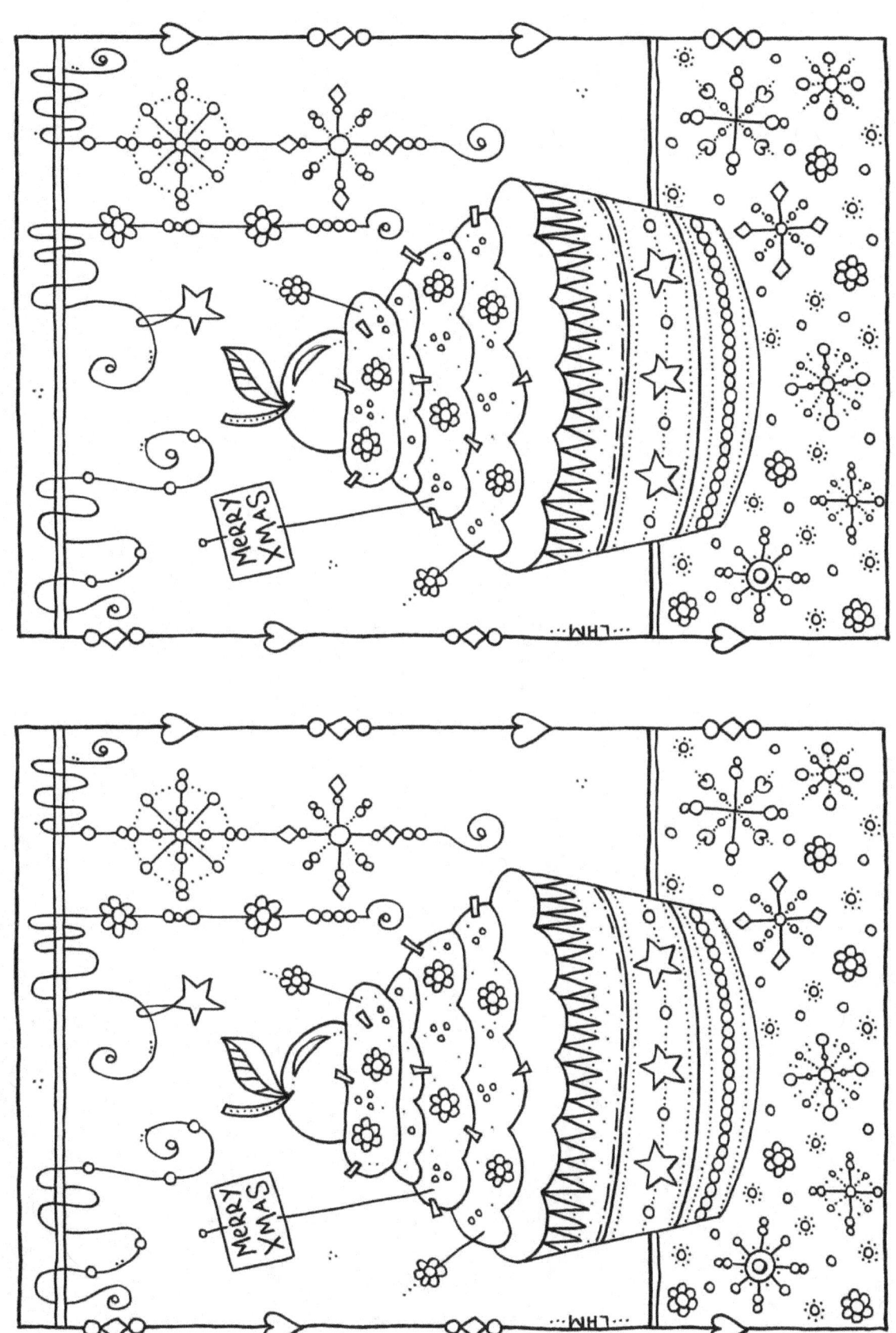

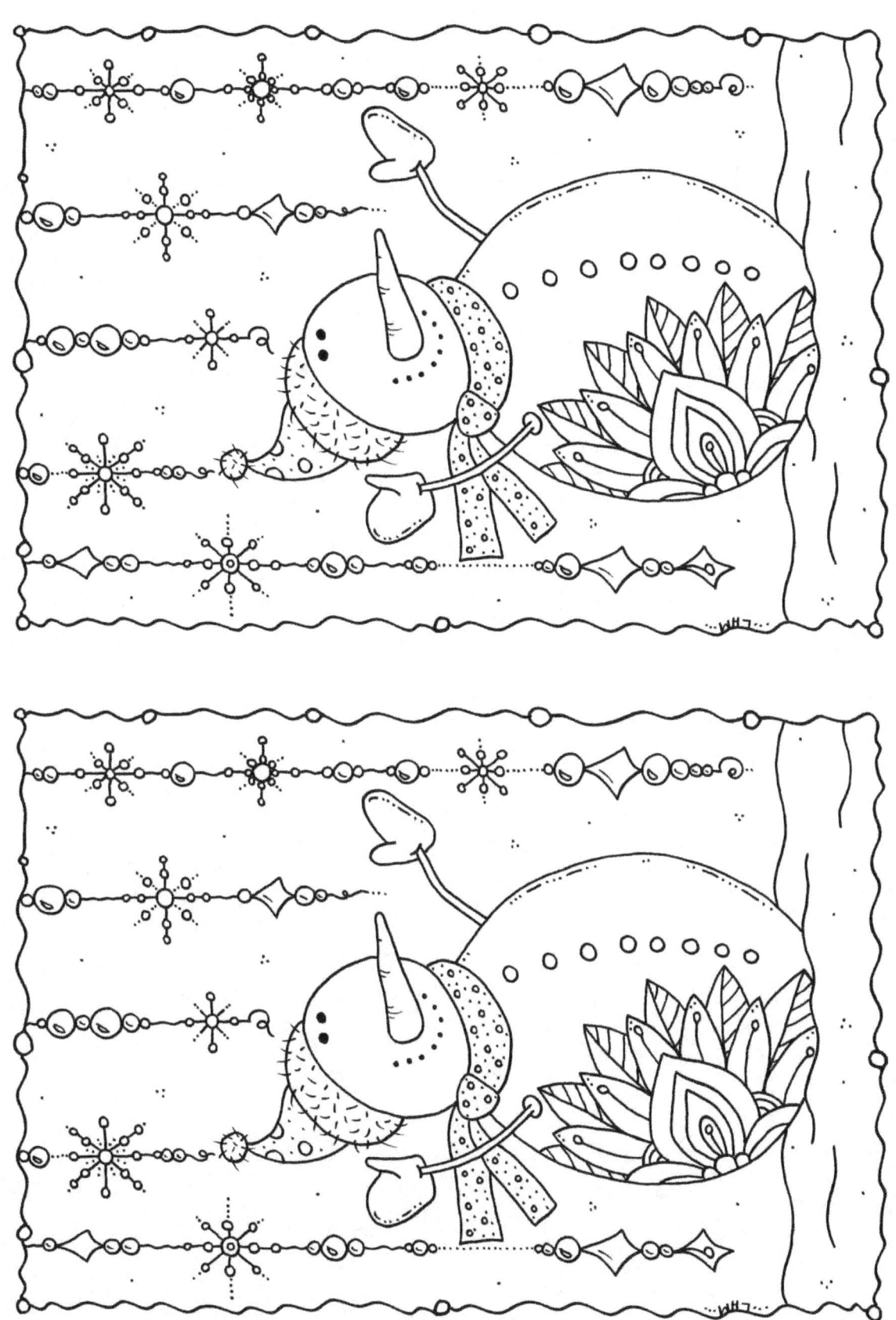

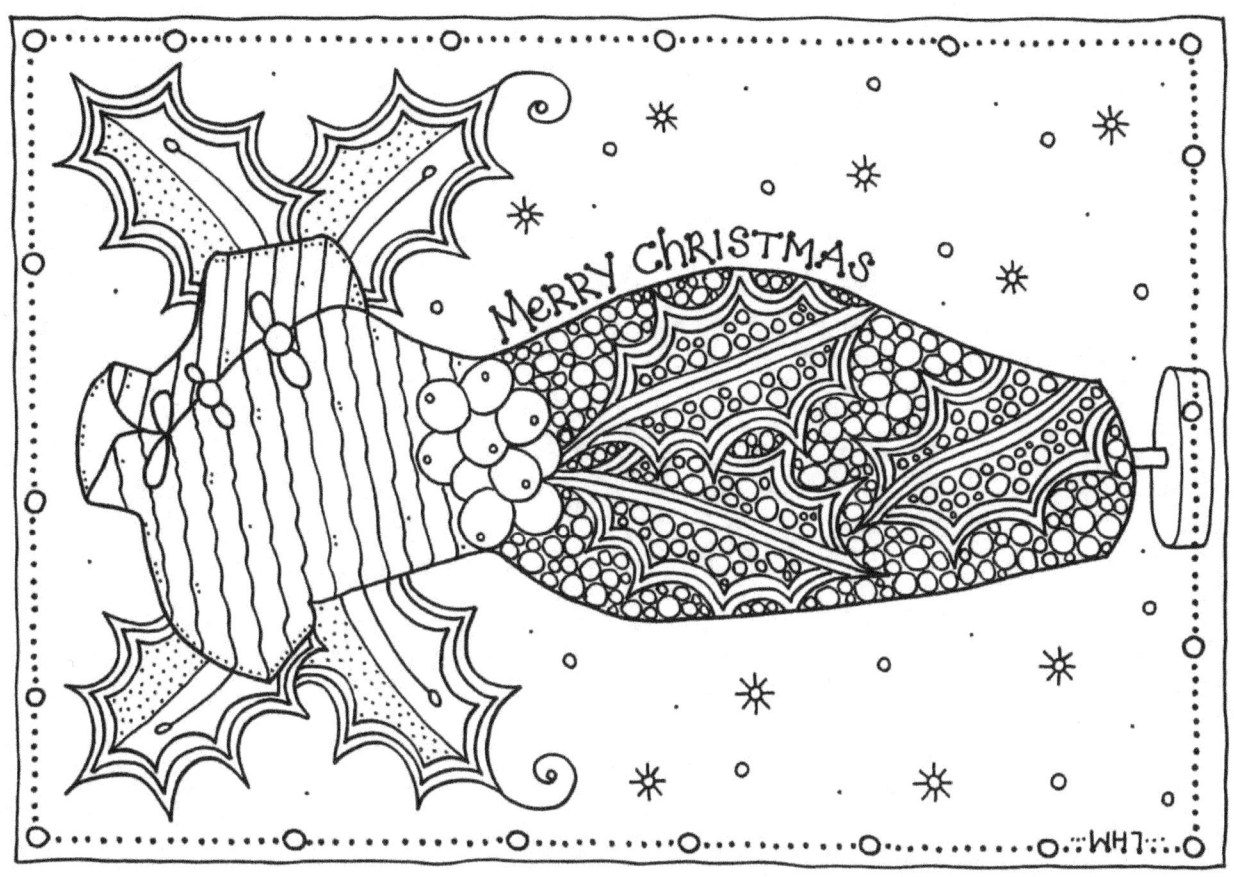

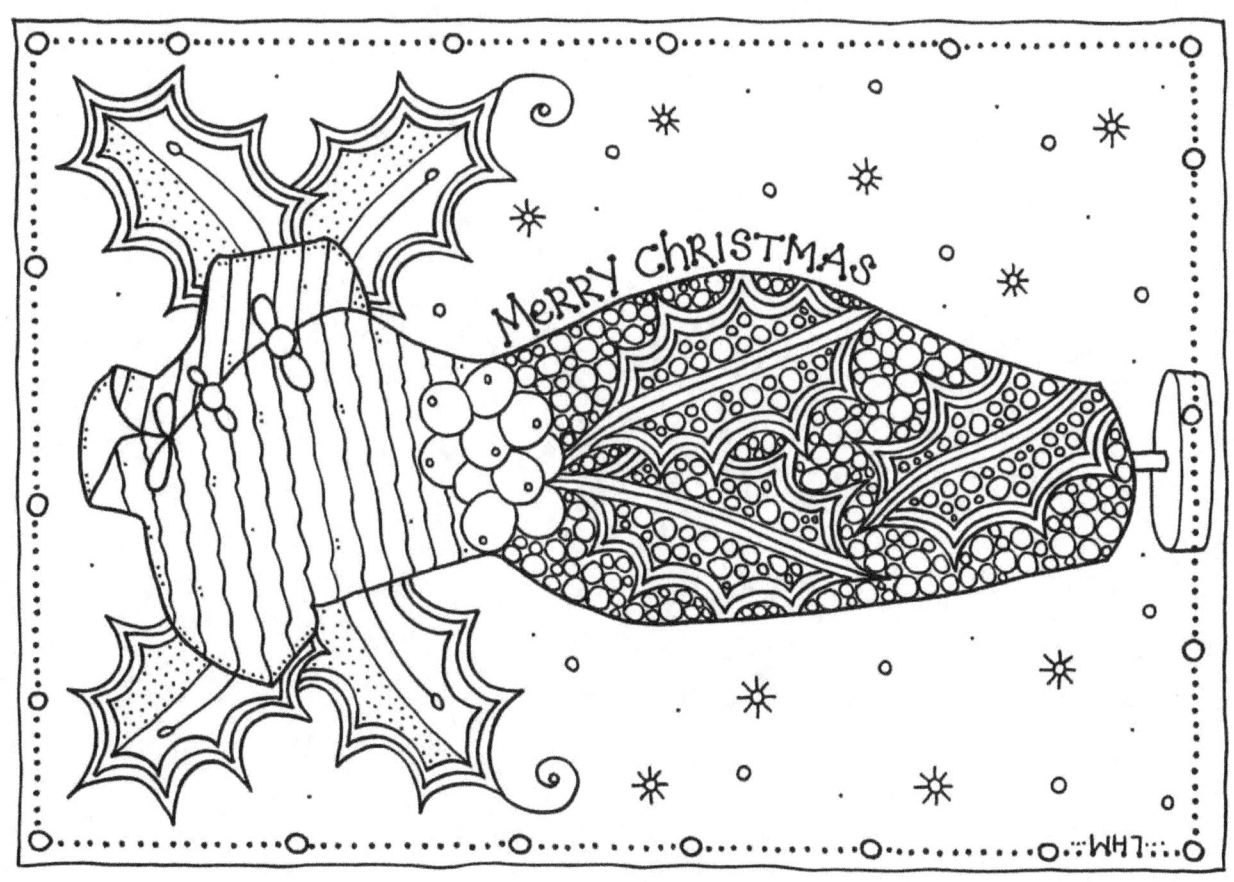

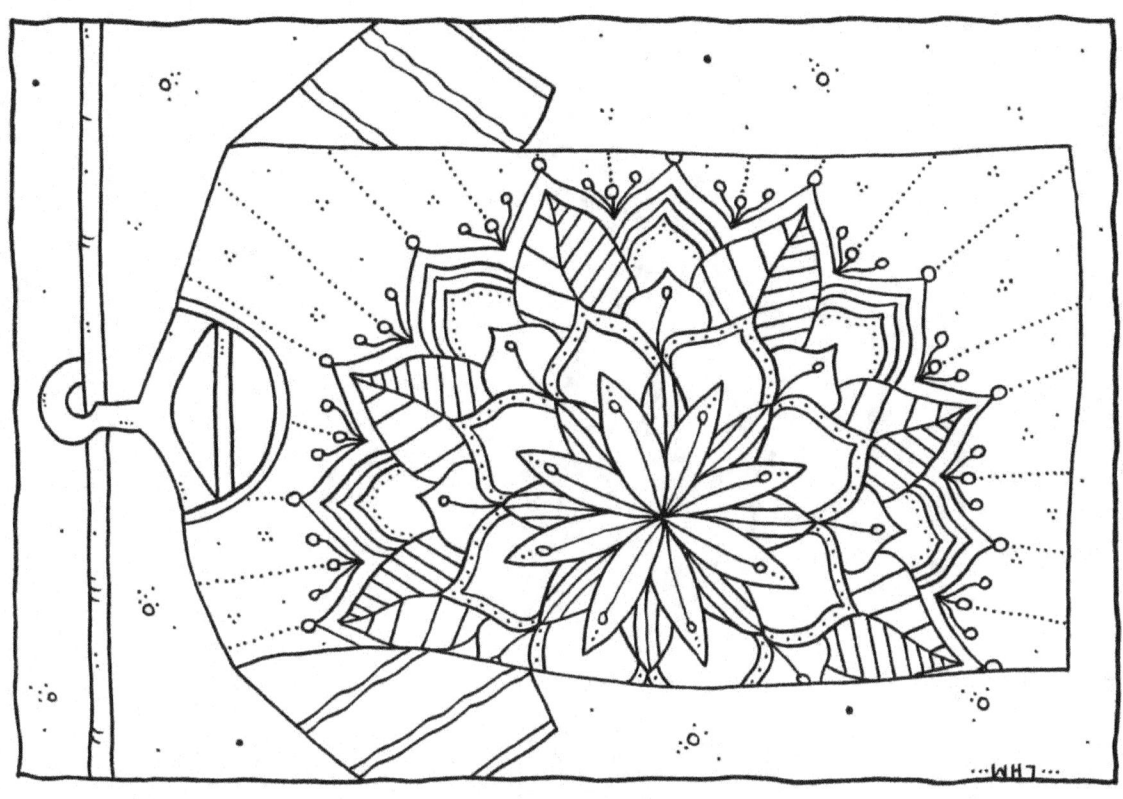
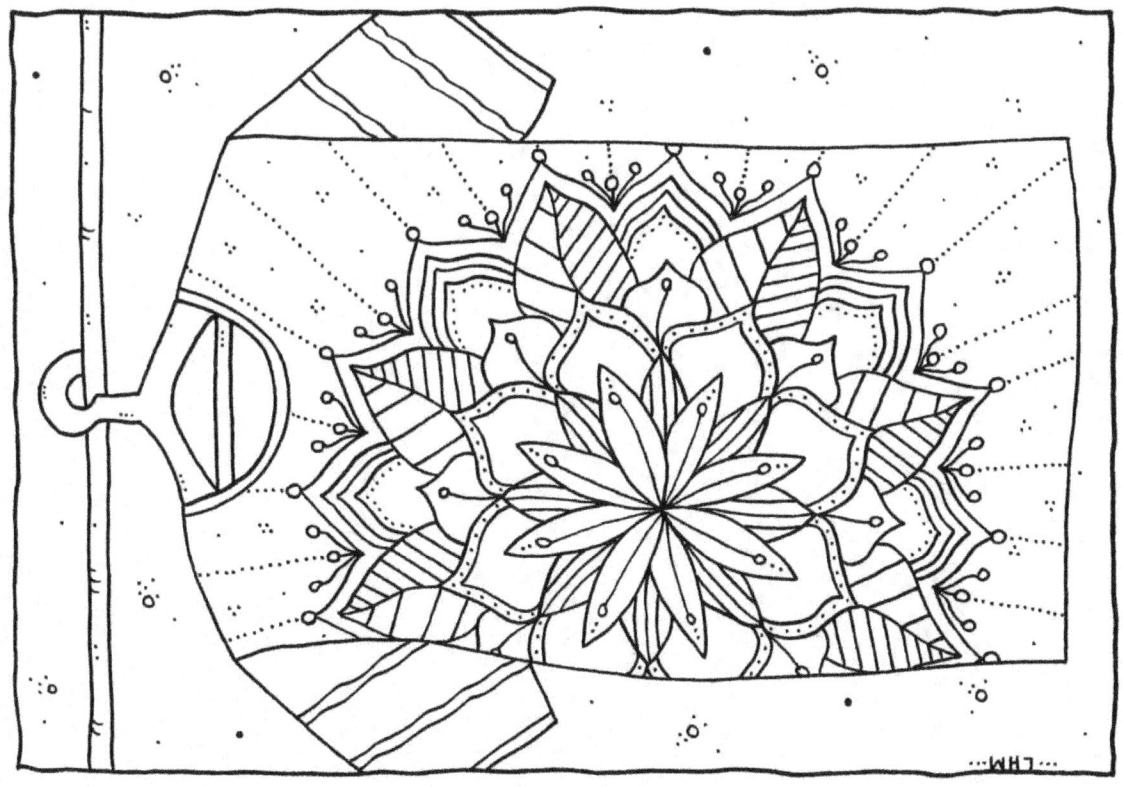

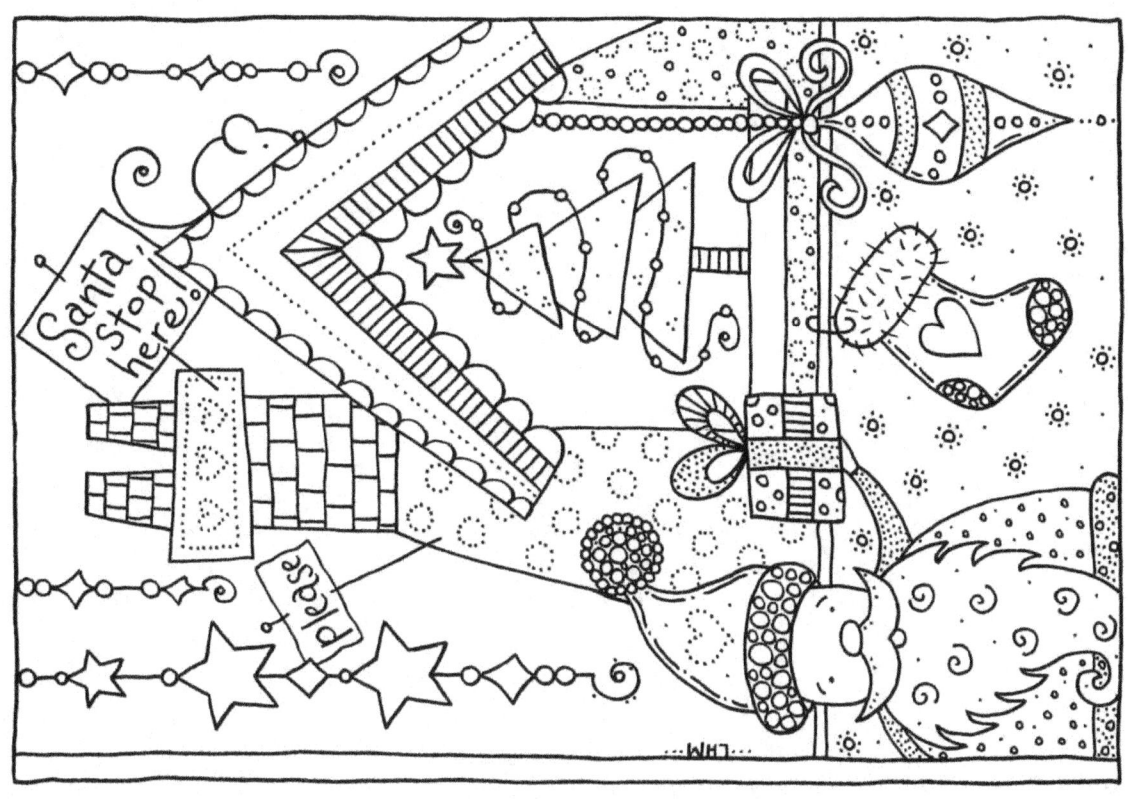
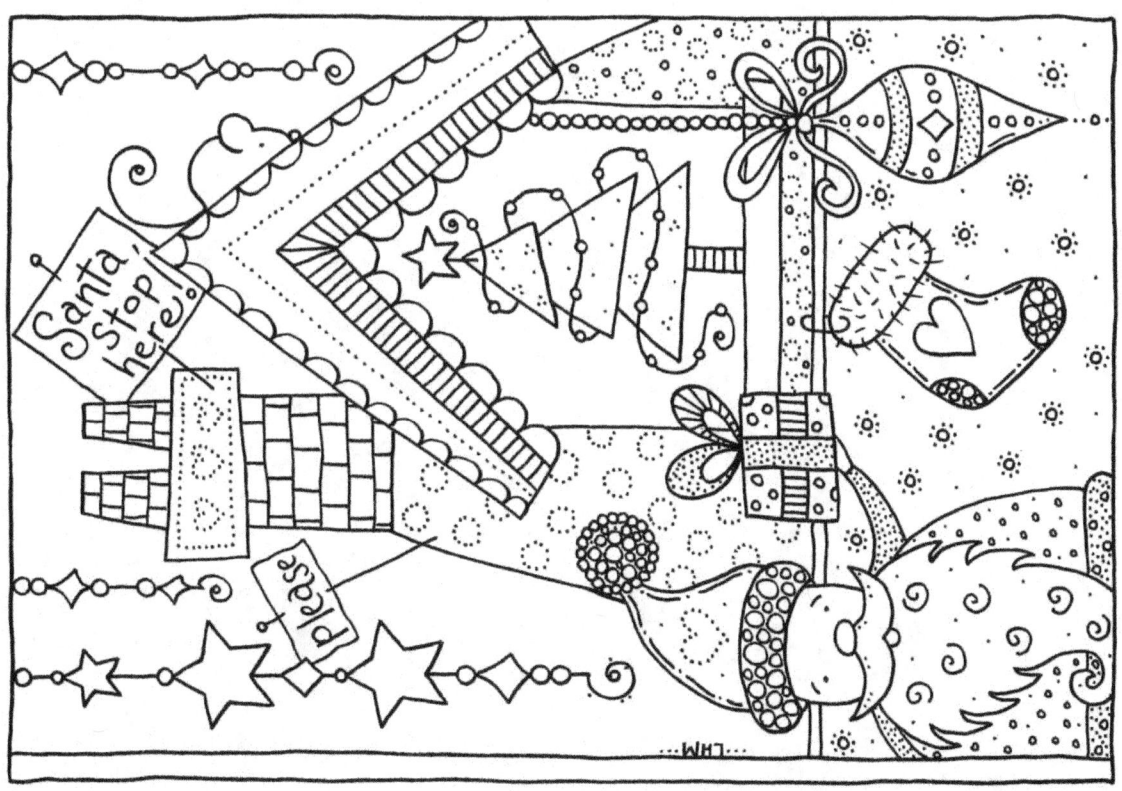

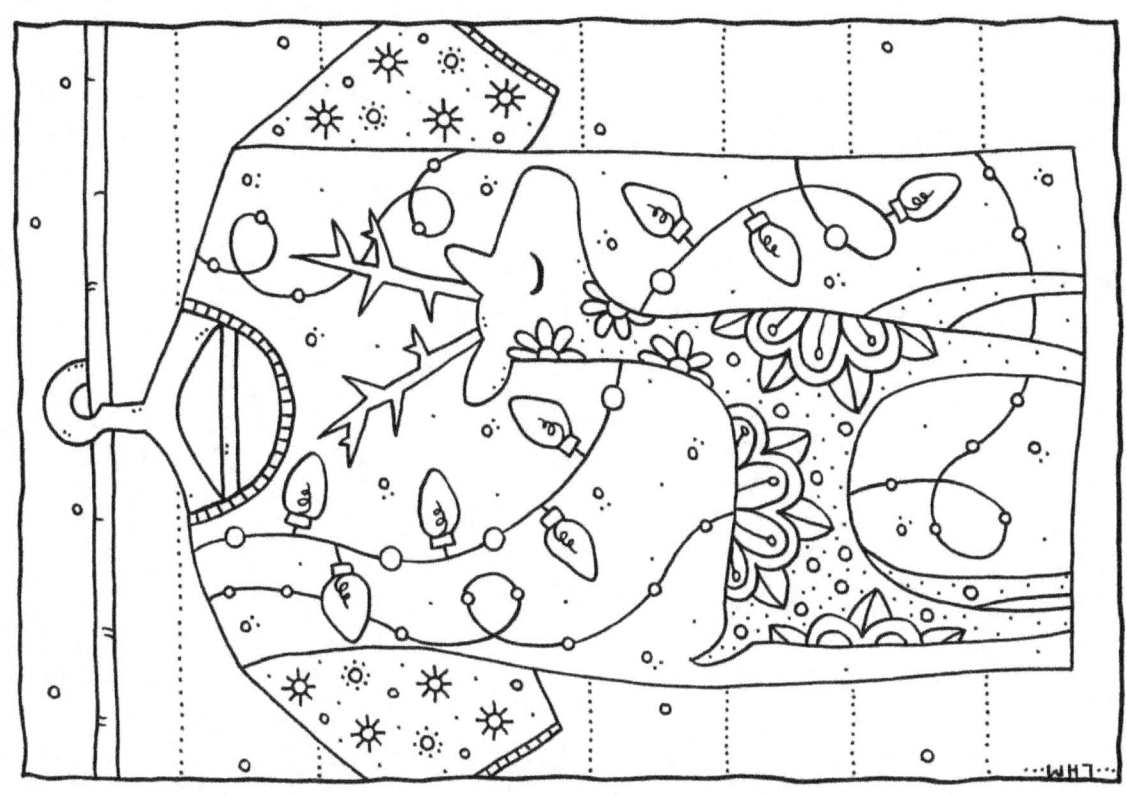
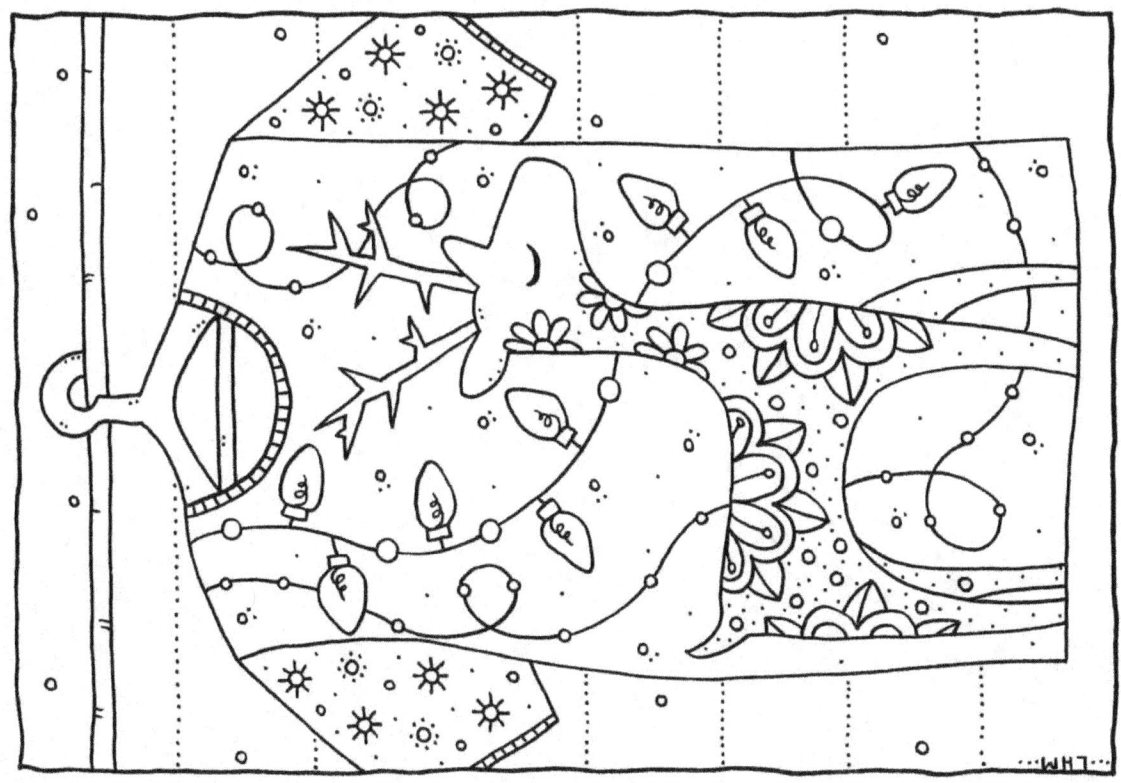

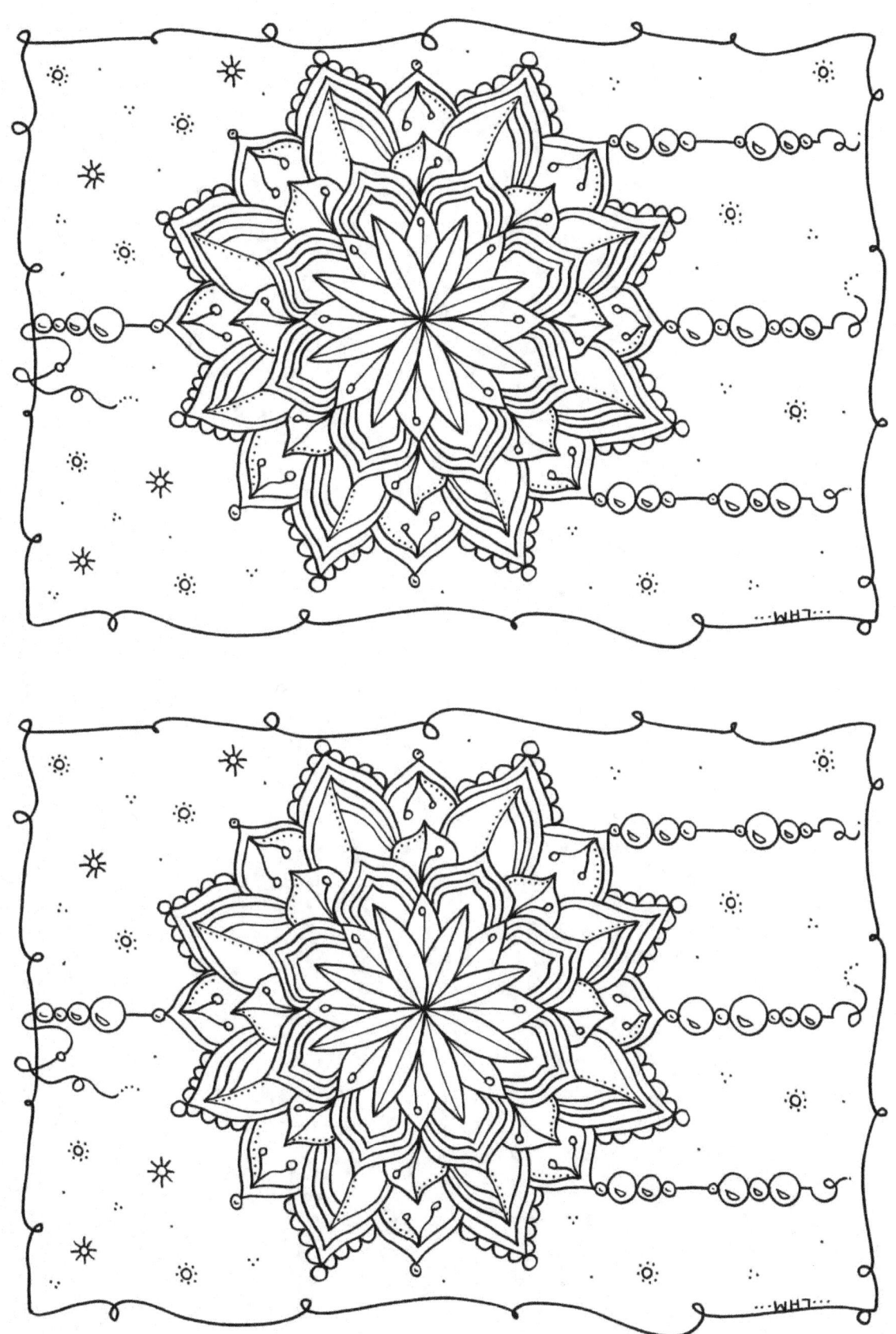

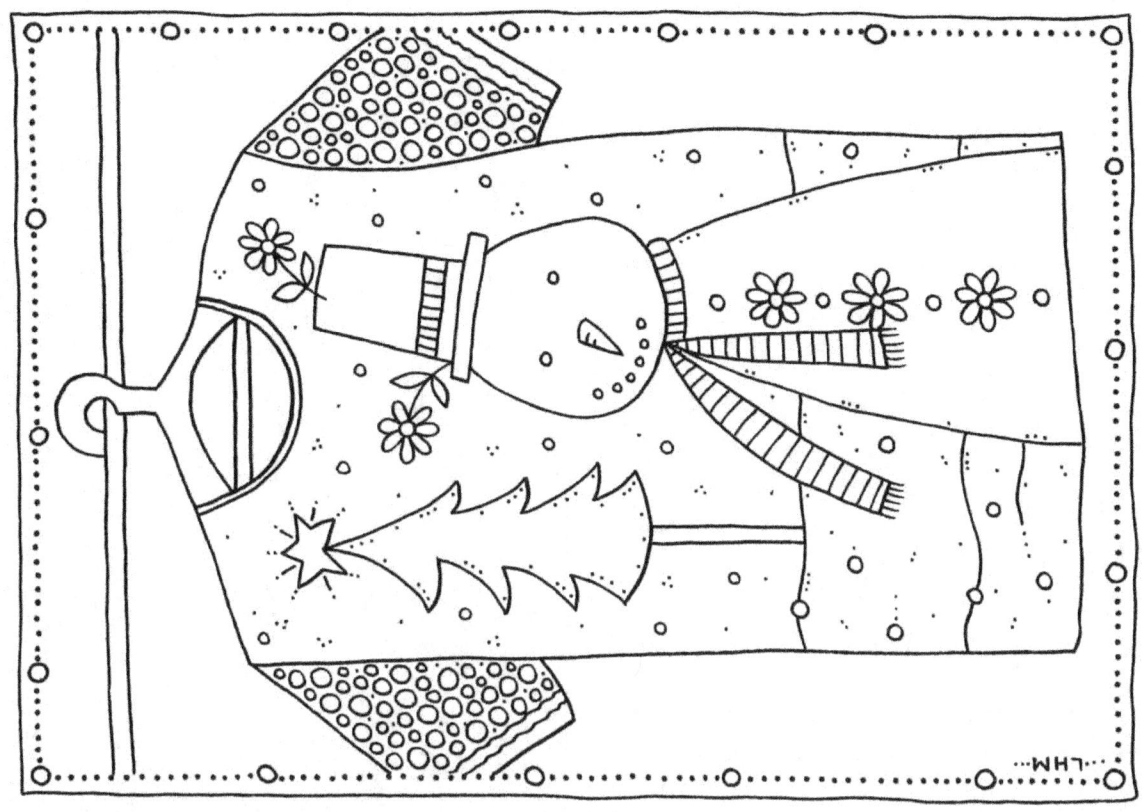
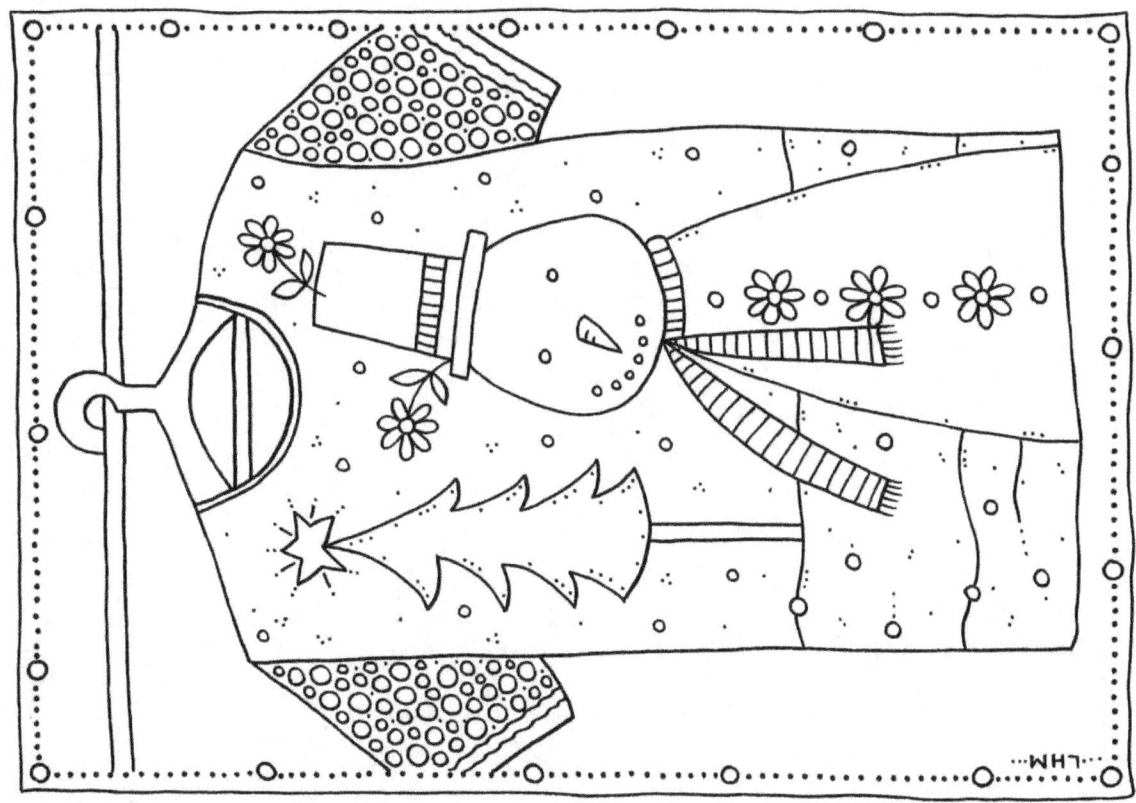

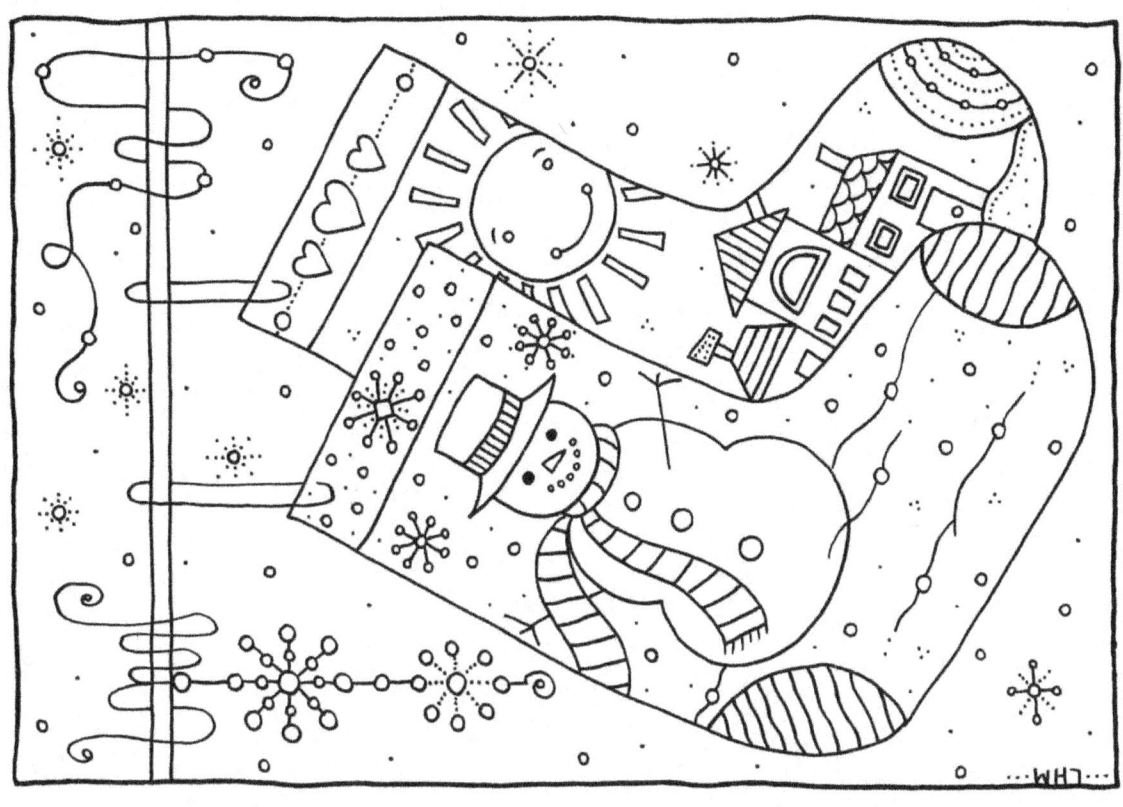
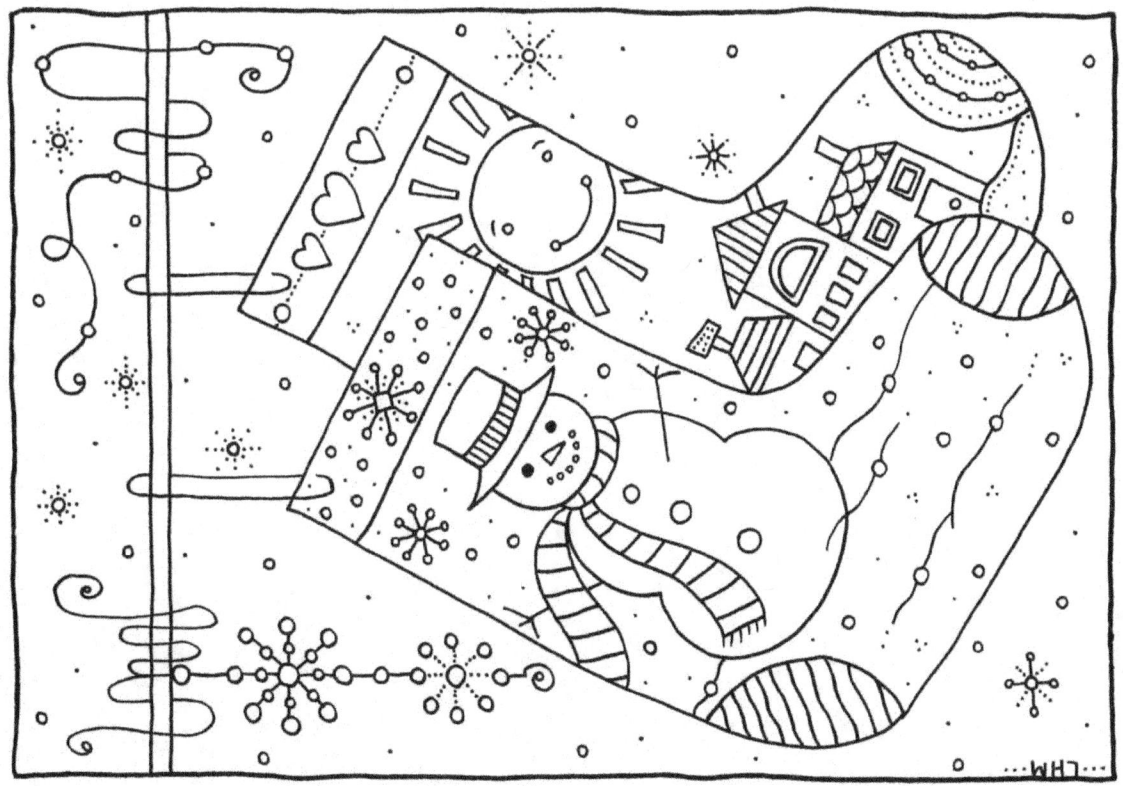

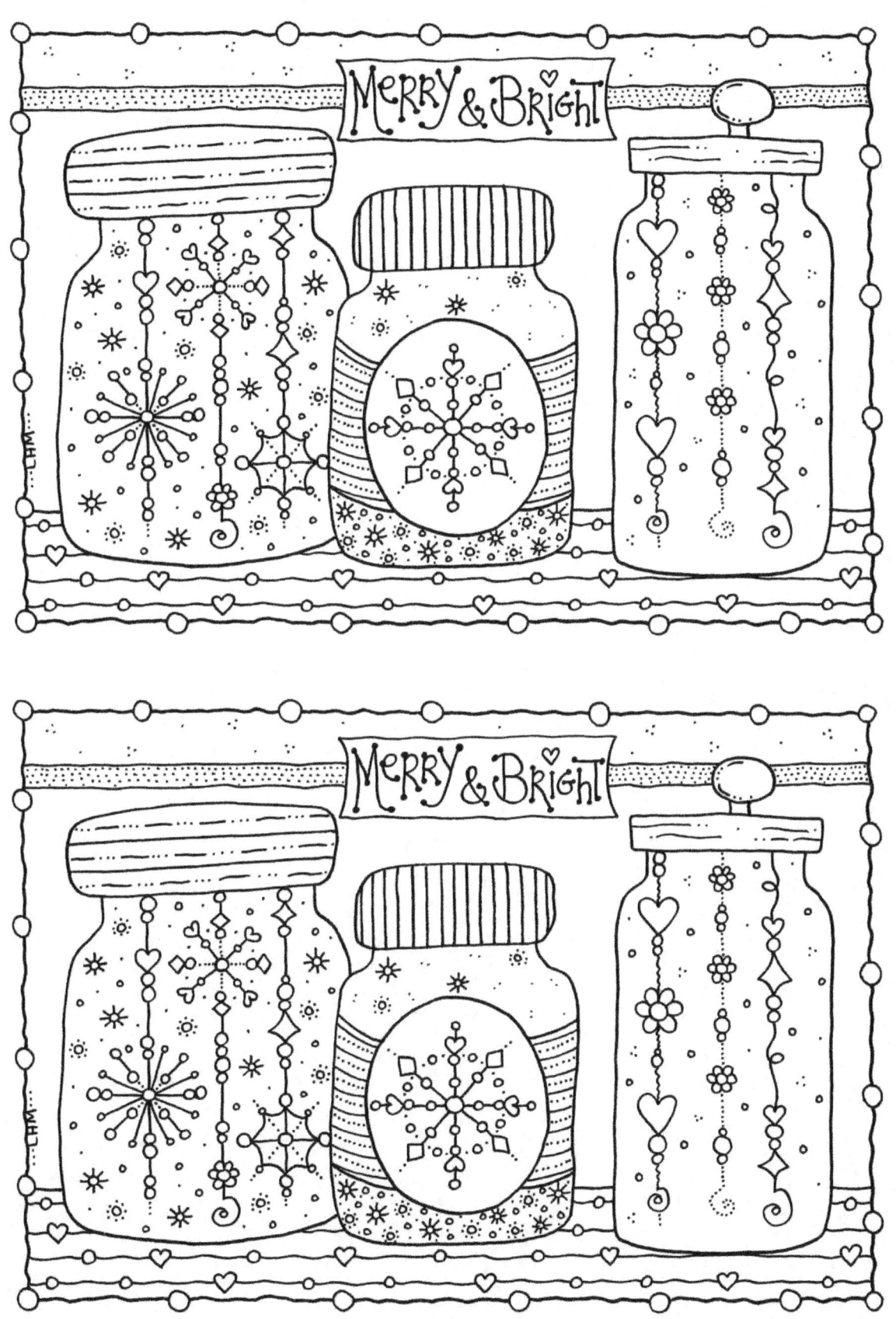

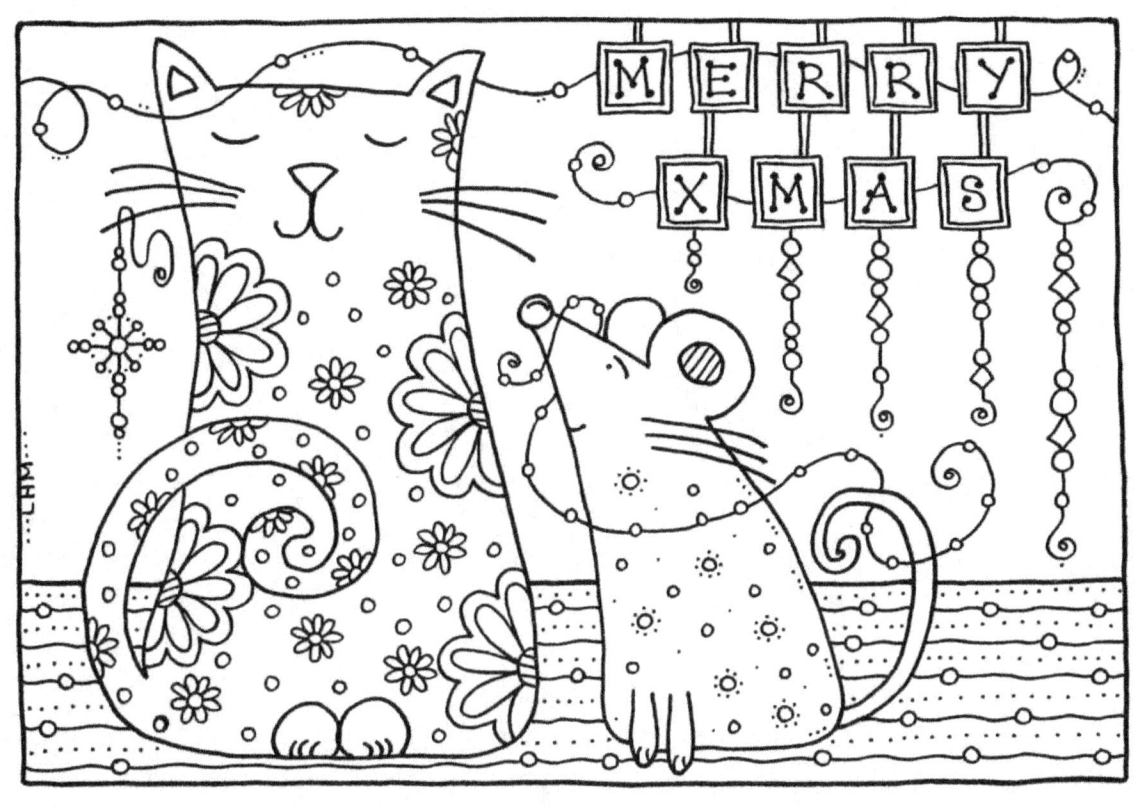
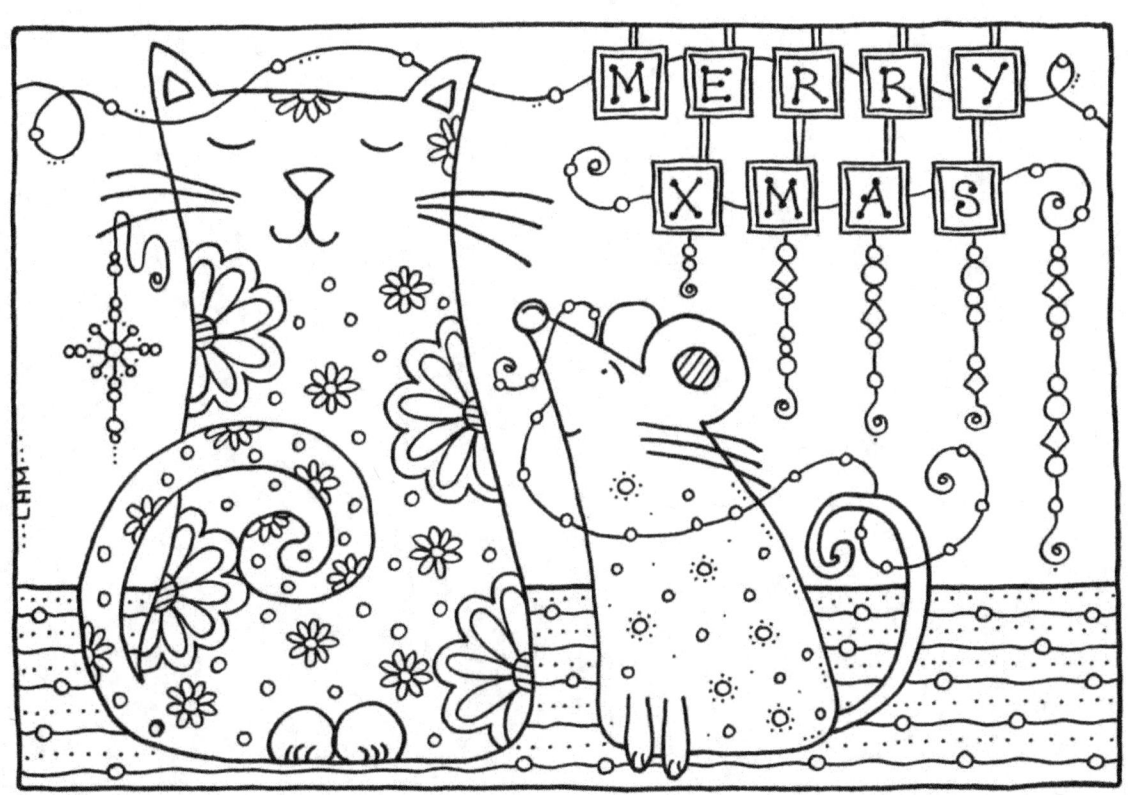

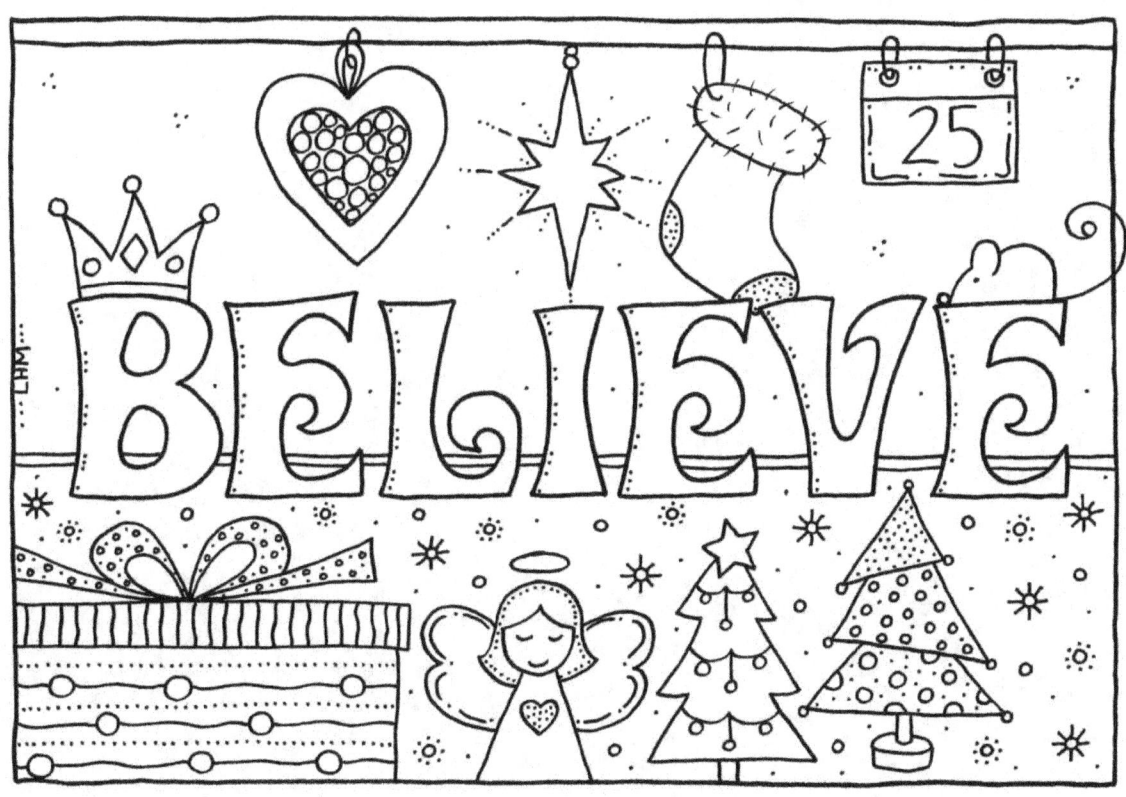

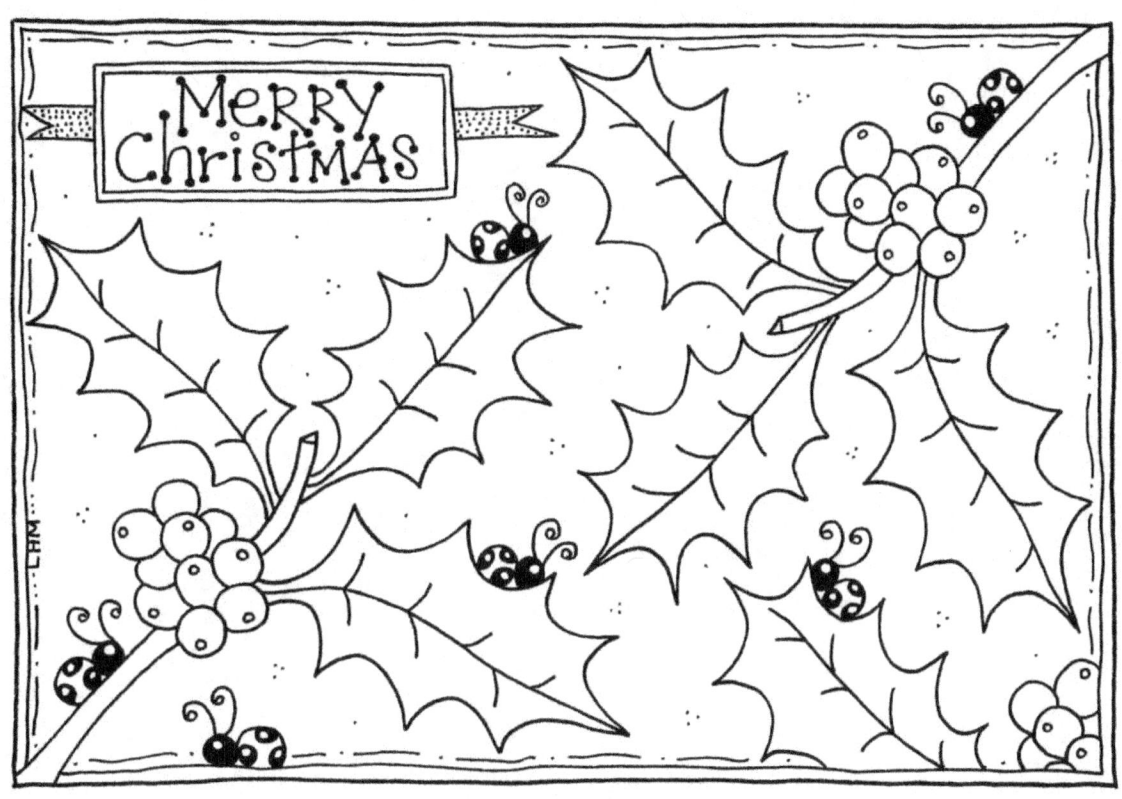
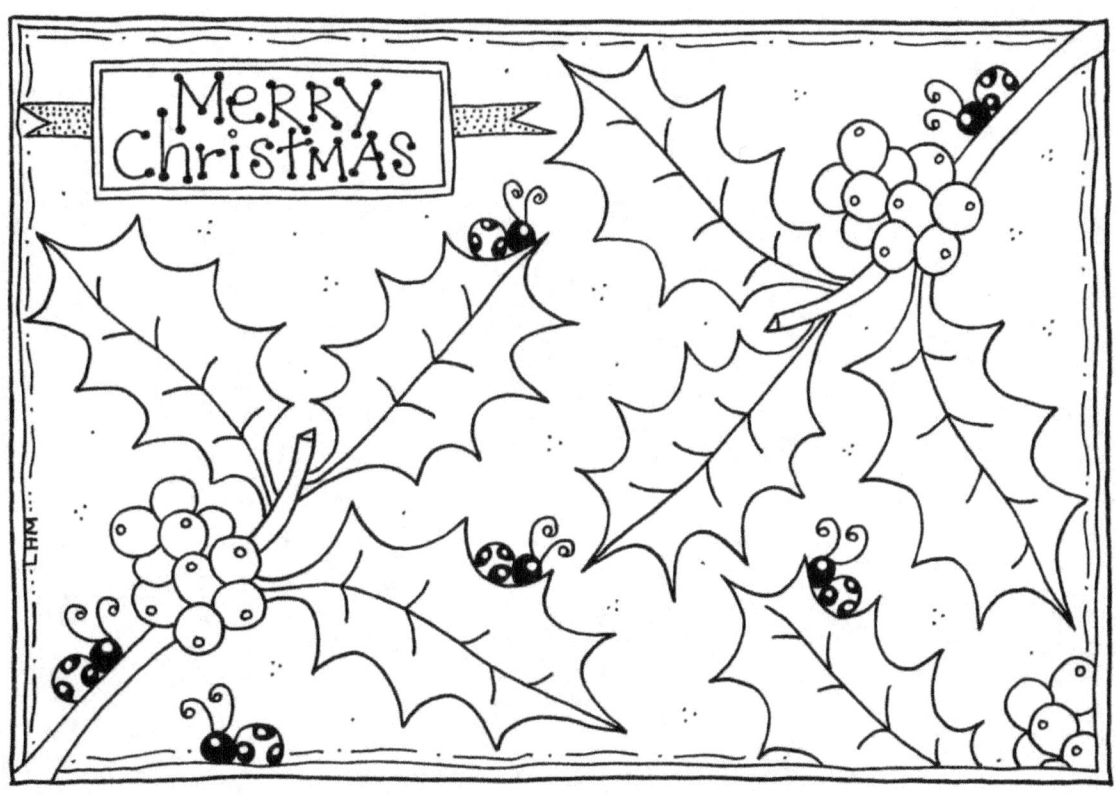

Card Topper images

The images in this section are all Card Topper - A6 sized.

You have my permission to photocopy them for your own personal use. They may not be used for commercial use without my prior written consent.

If you would like to make these into cards either use the original images from the book, or photocopy them onto thin card or paper first. After coloring mount them onto a folded A5 card with stick glue and a brayer, or double-sided tape.

You can then add embellishments. Glitter, washi tape, rubber stamping, 3D embellishments, ribbon, bows etc. Have fun, and experiment.

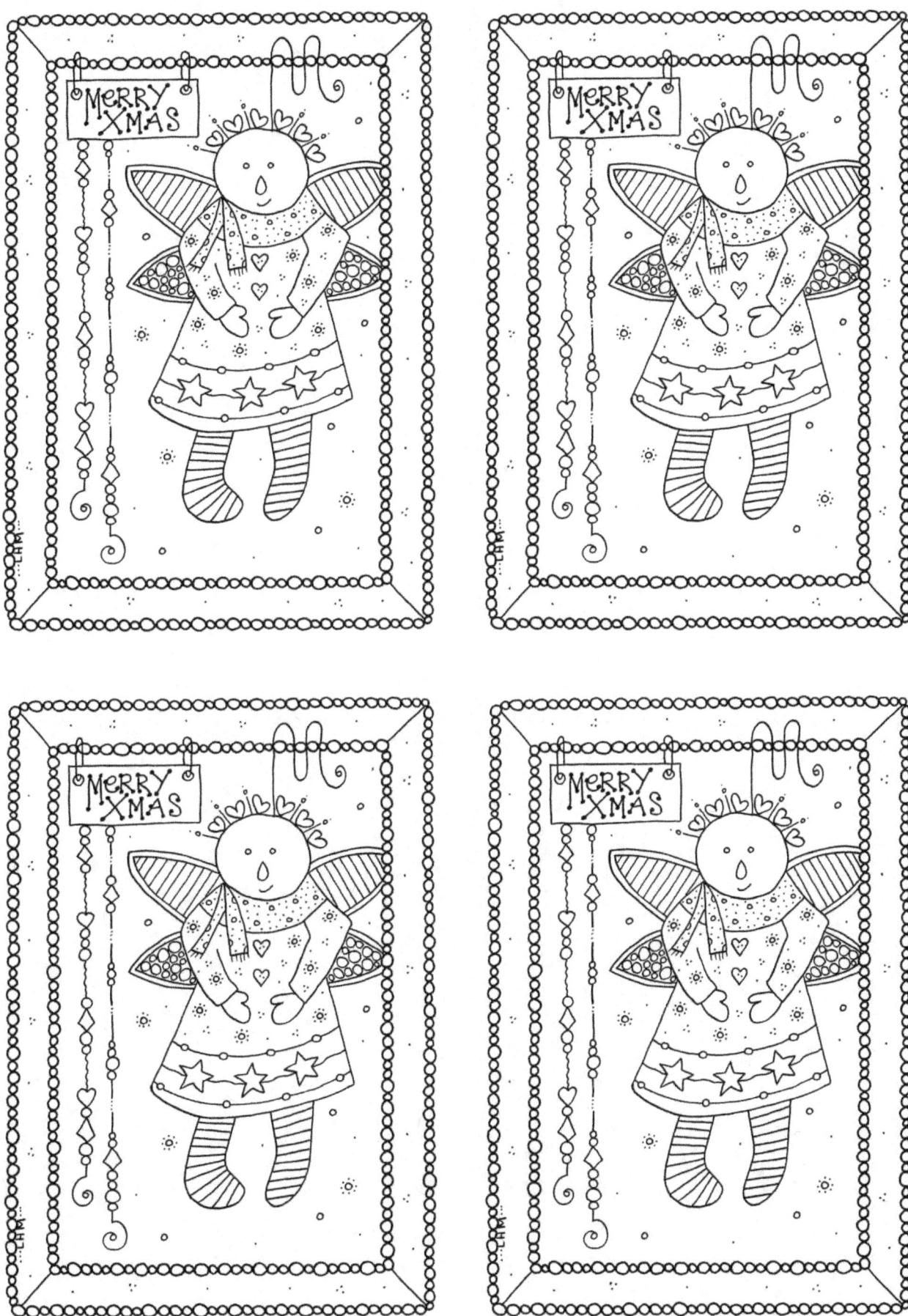

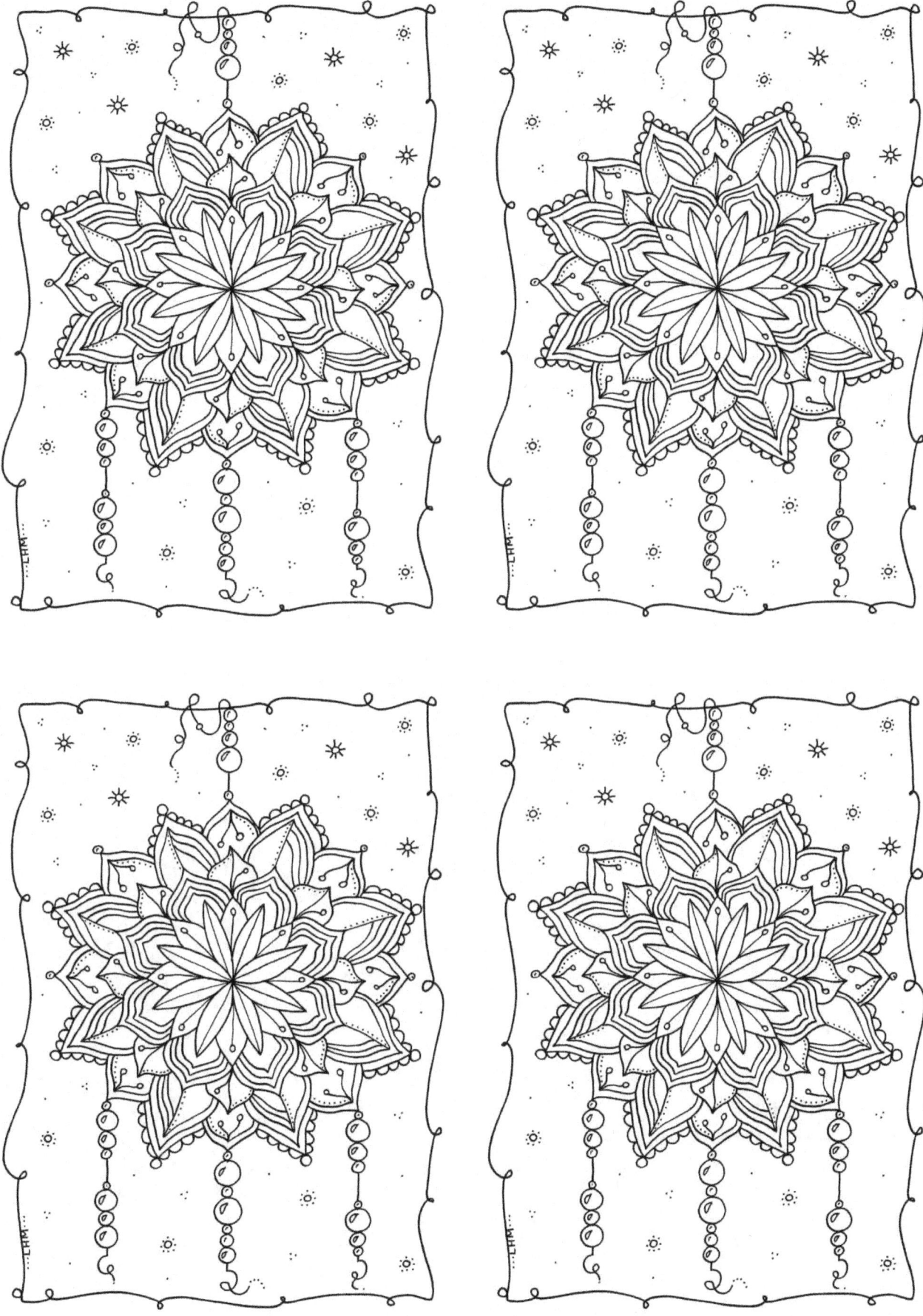

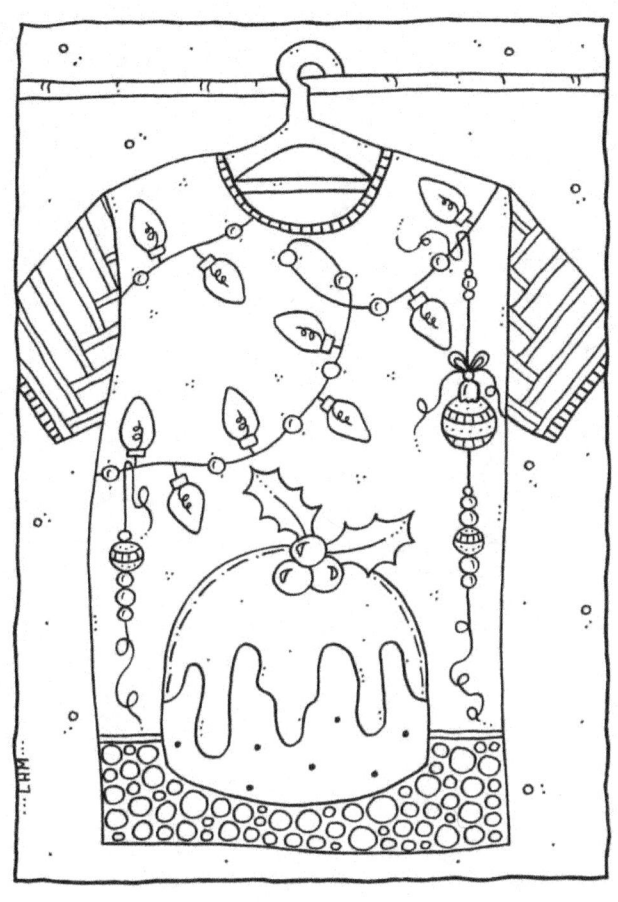
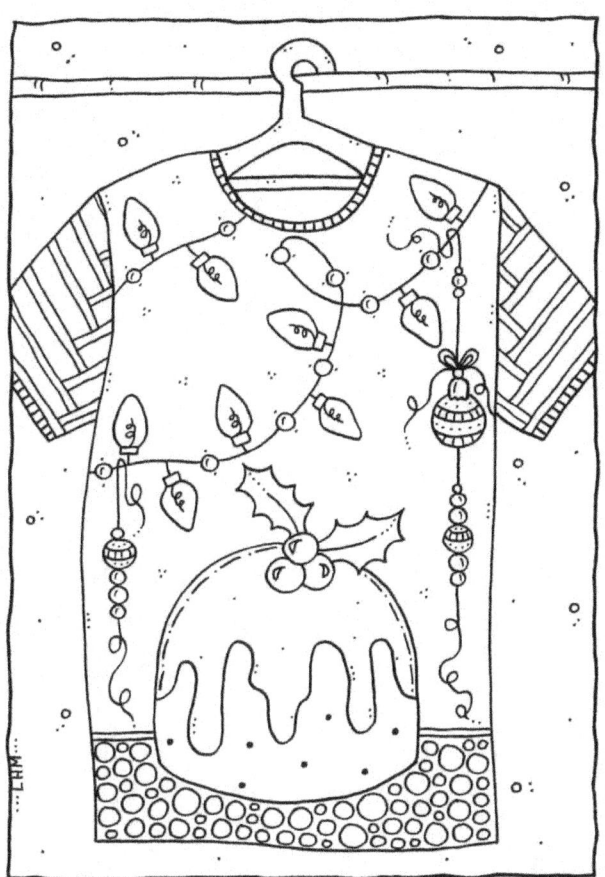
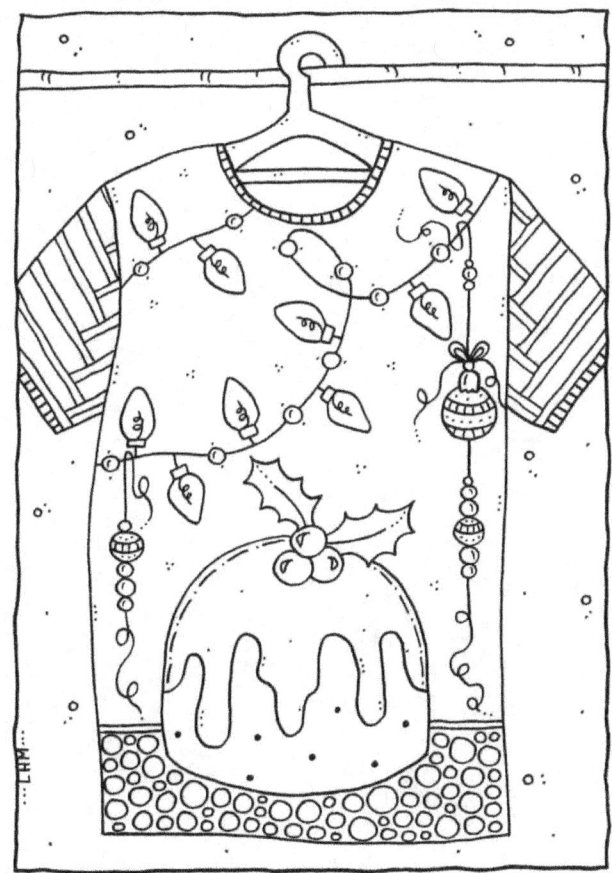
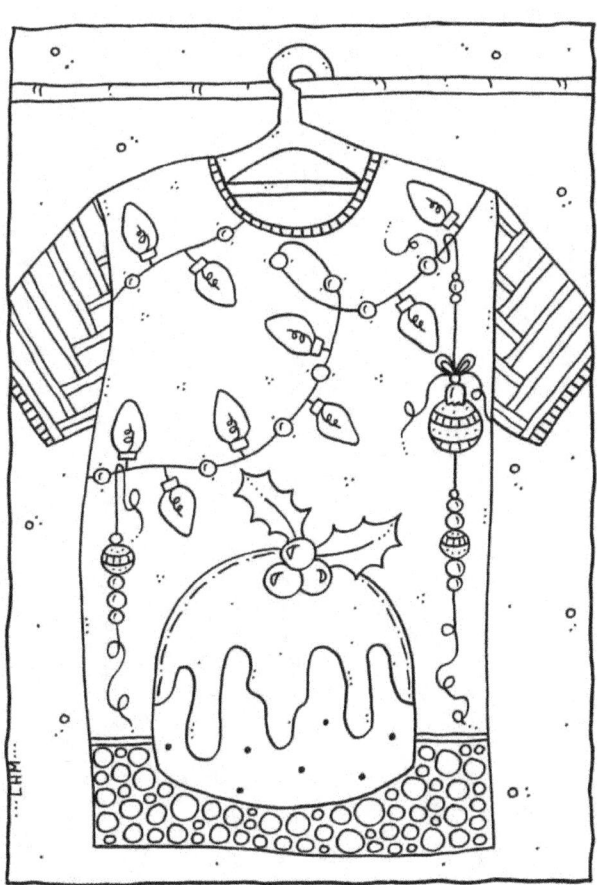

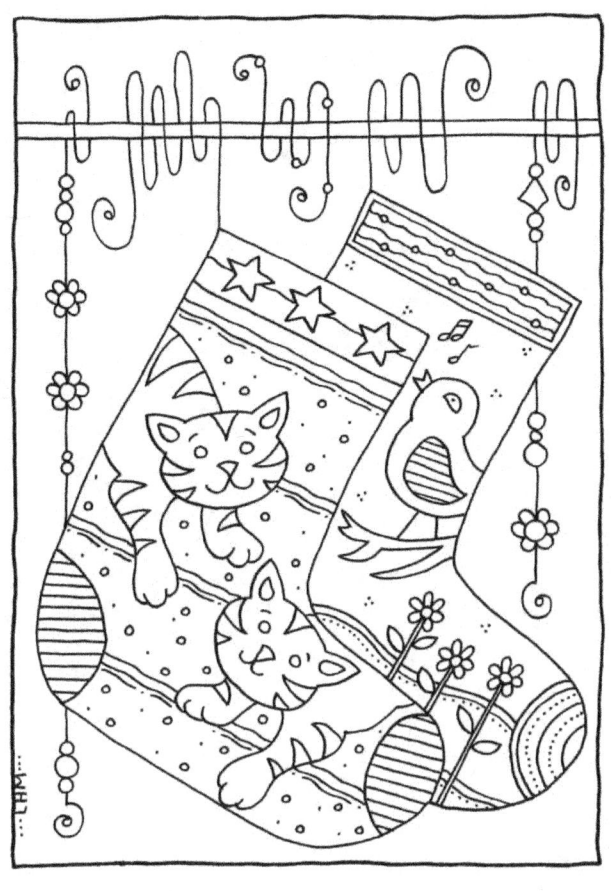
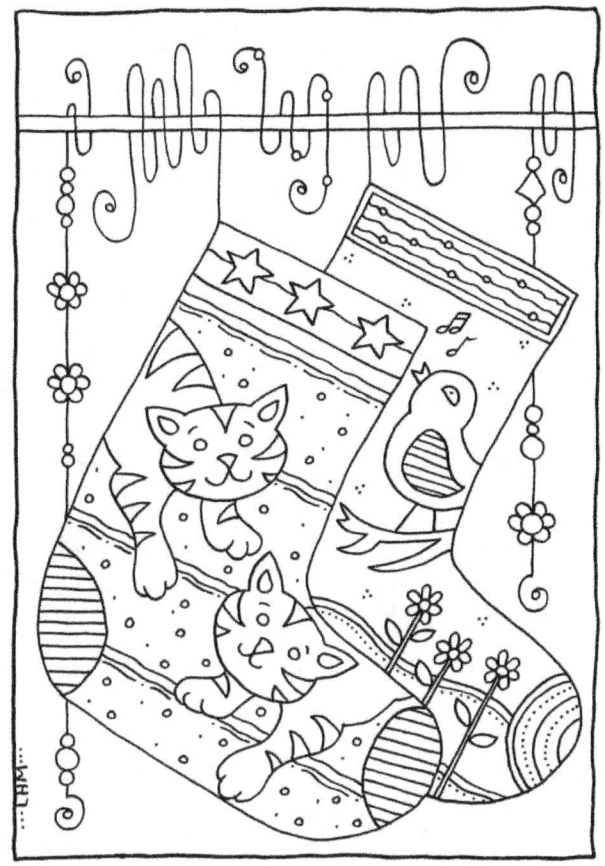
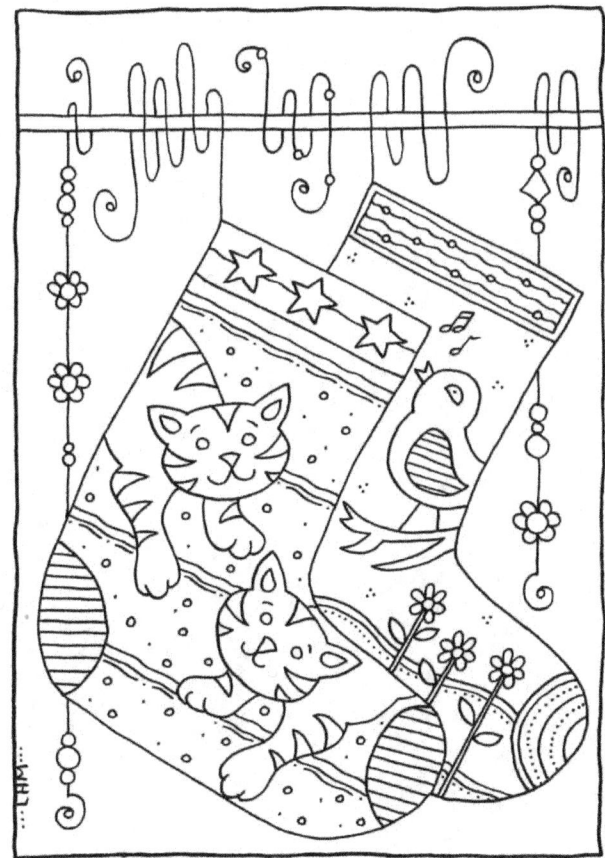
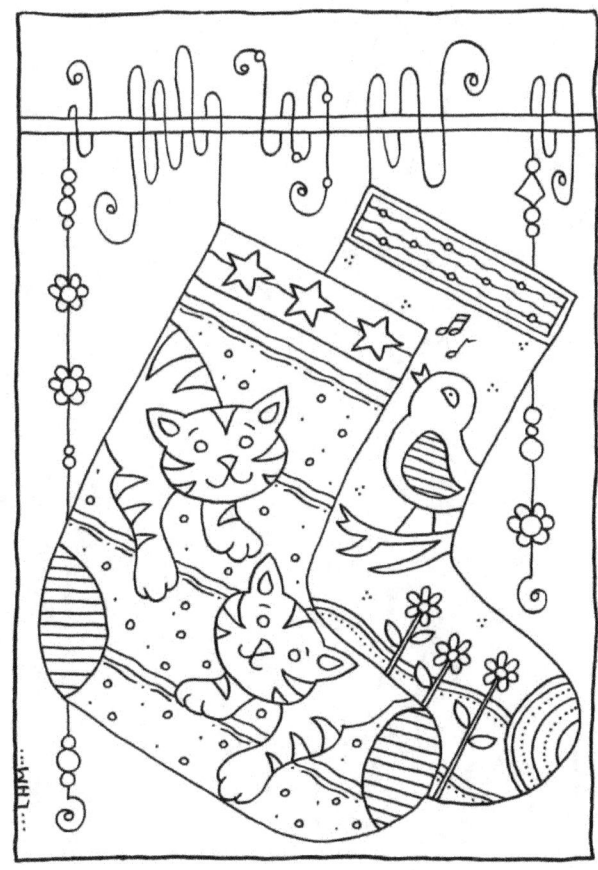

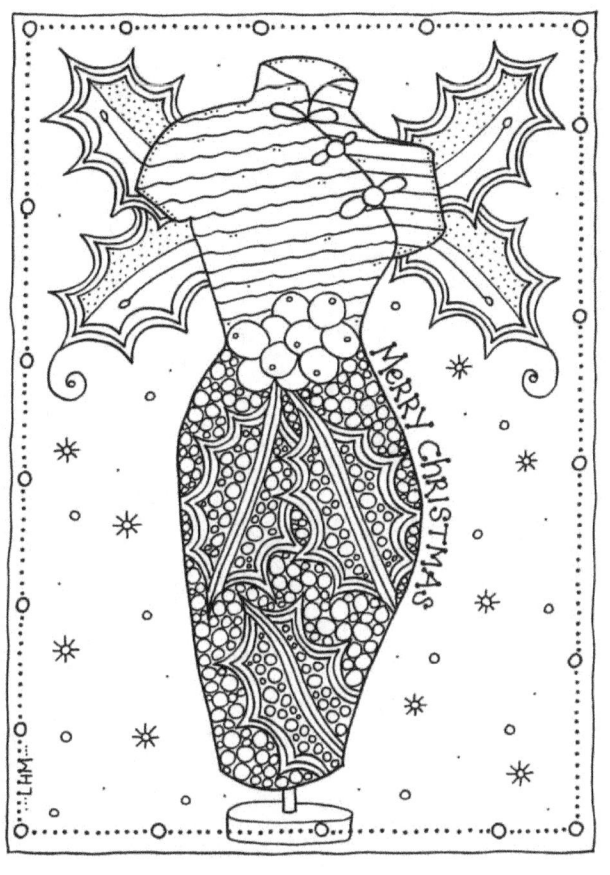
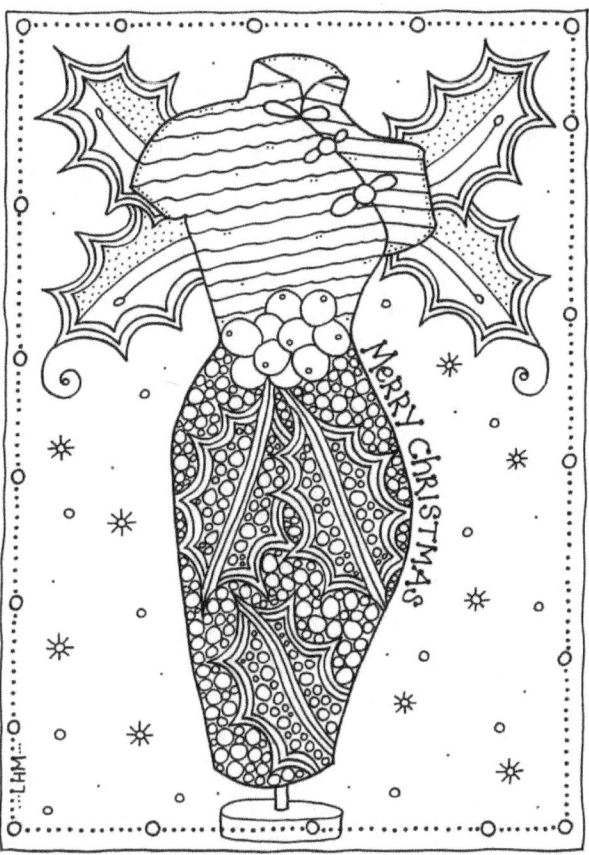
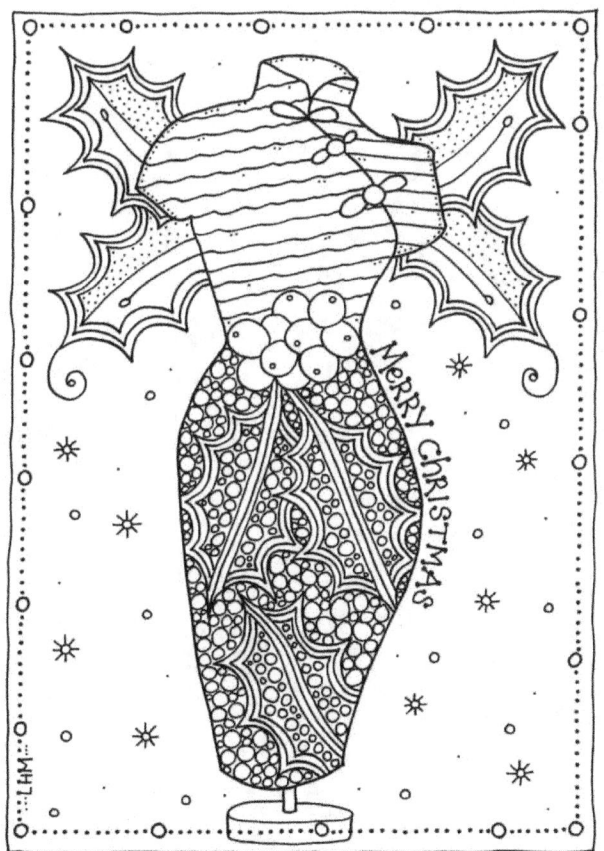
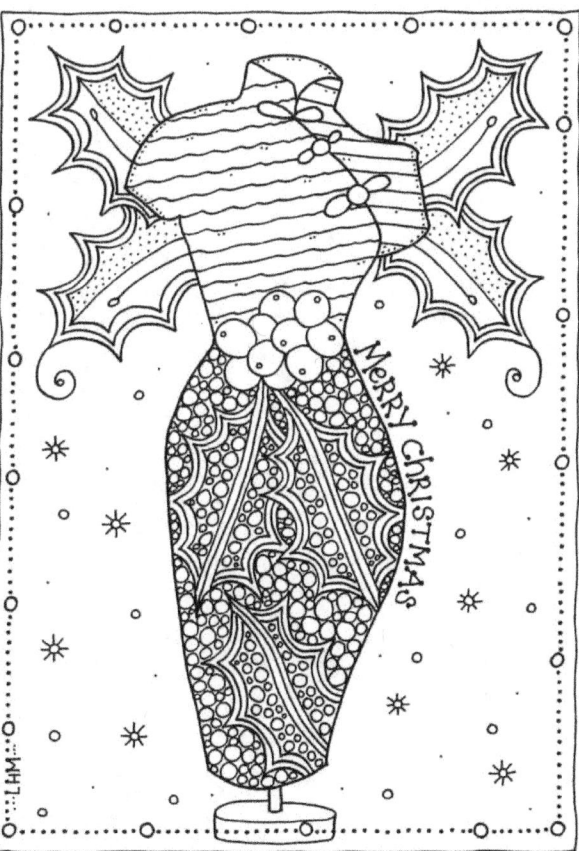

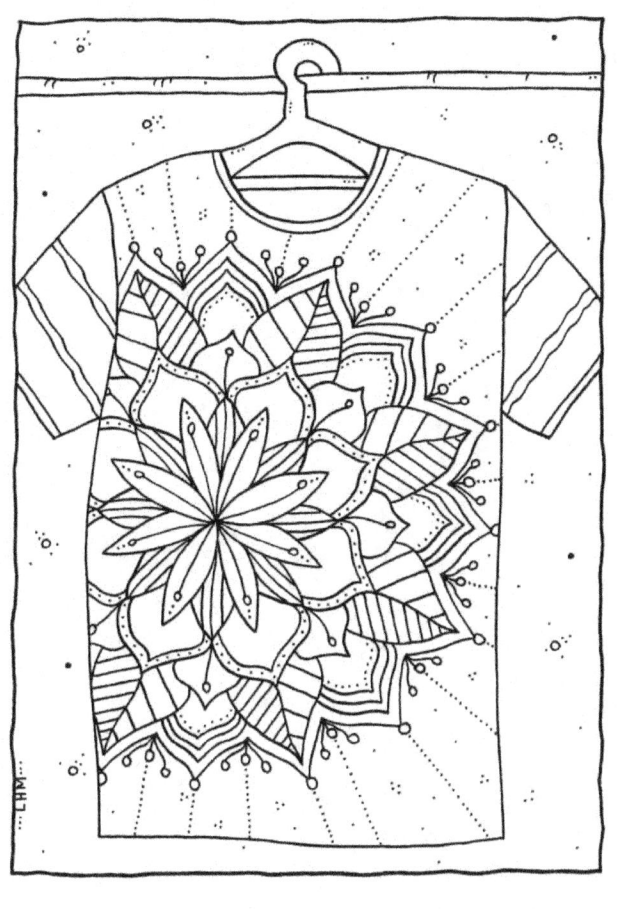
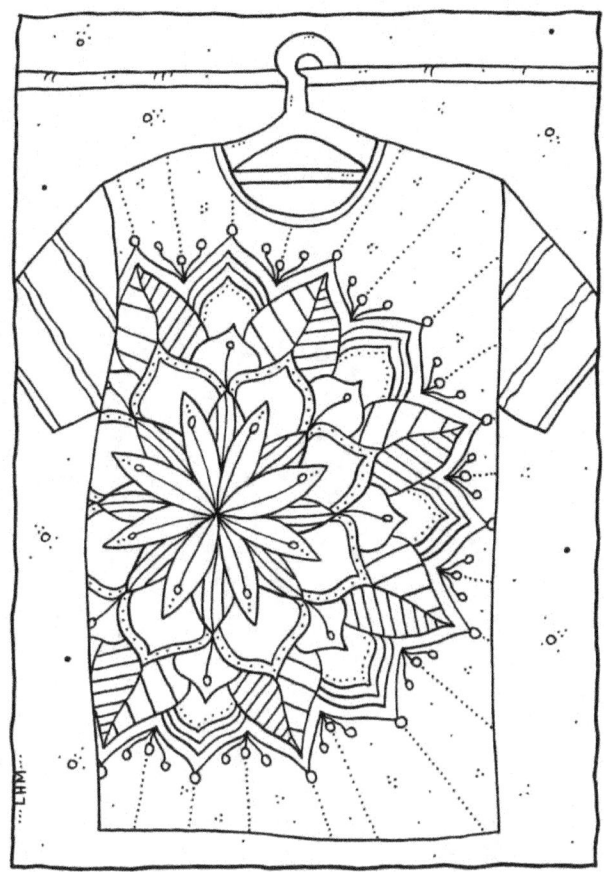
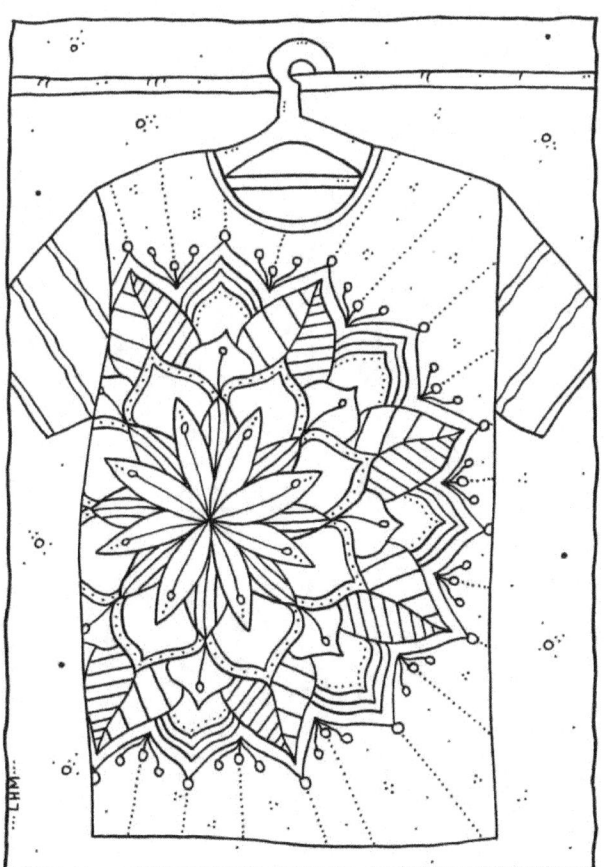
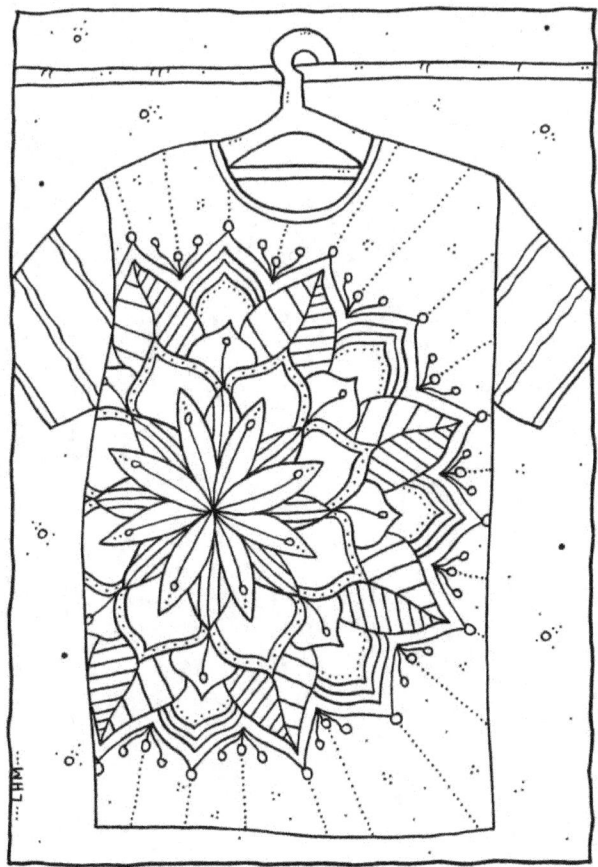

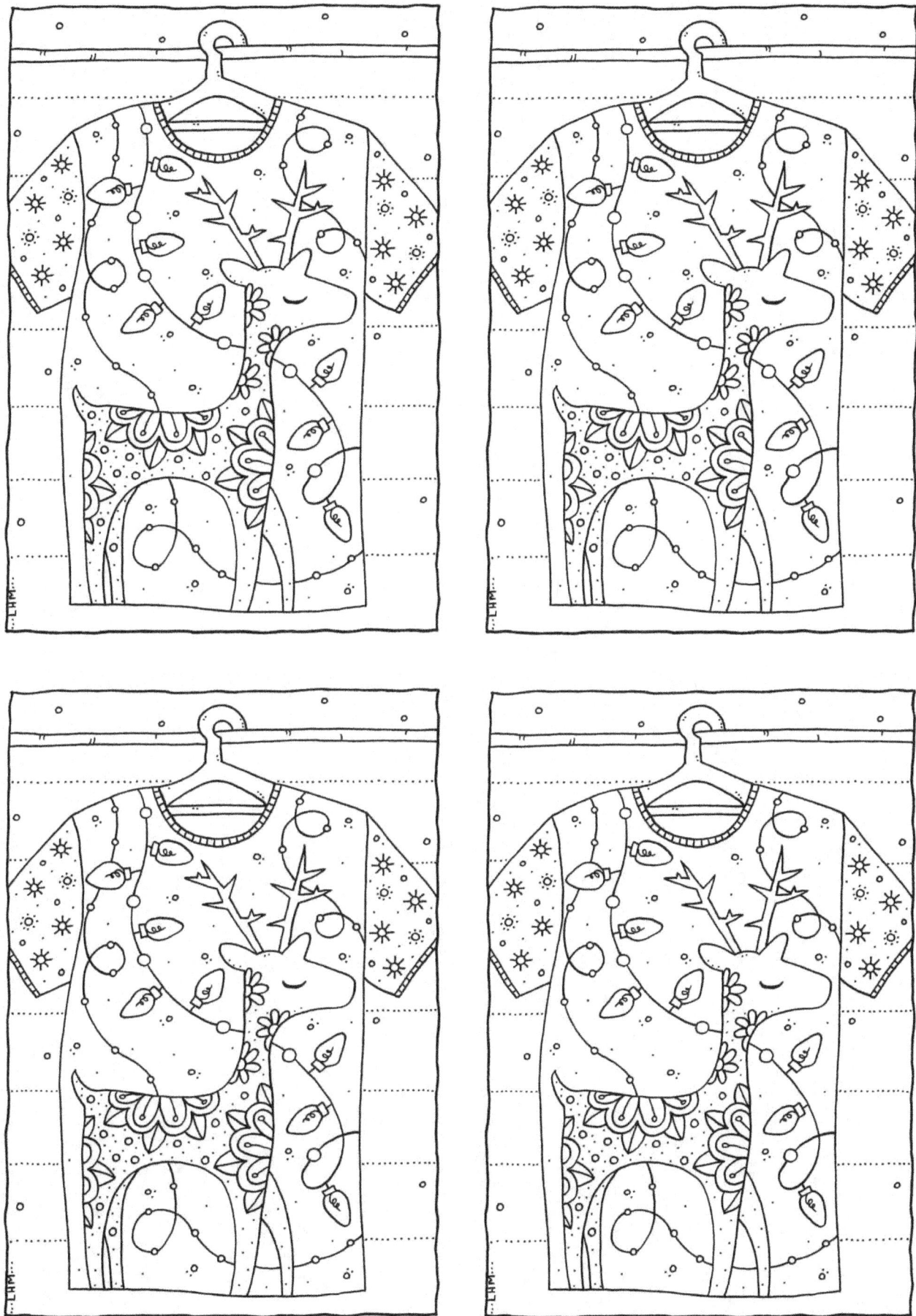

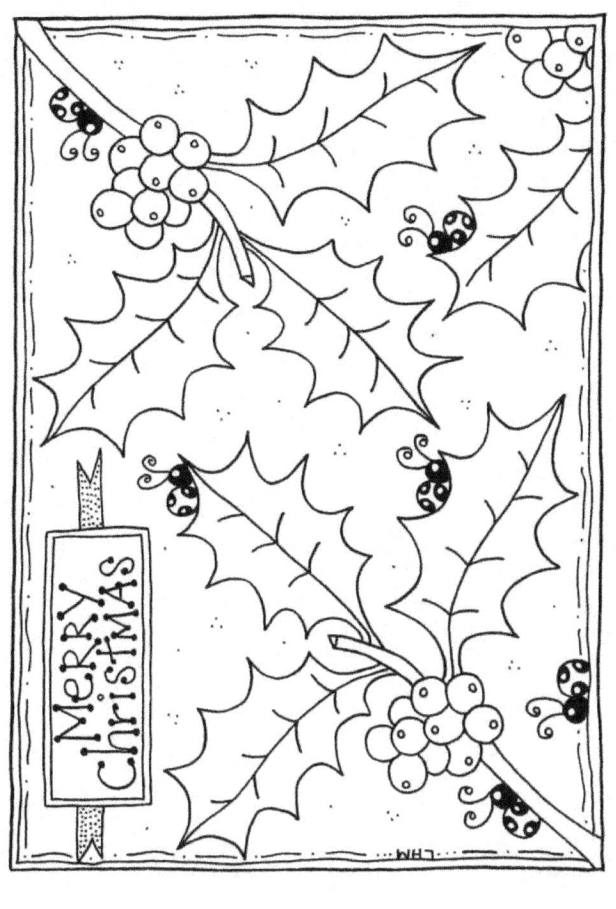
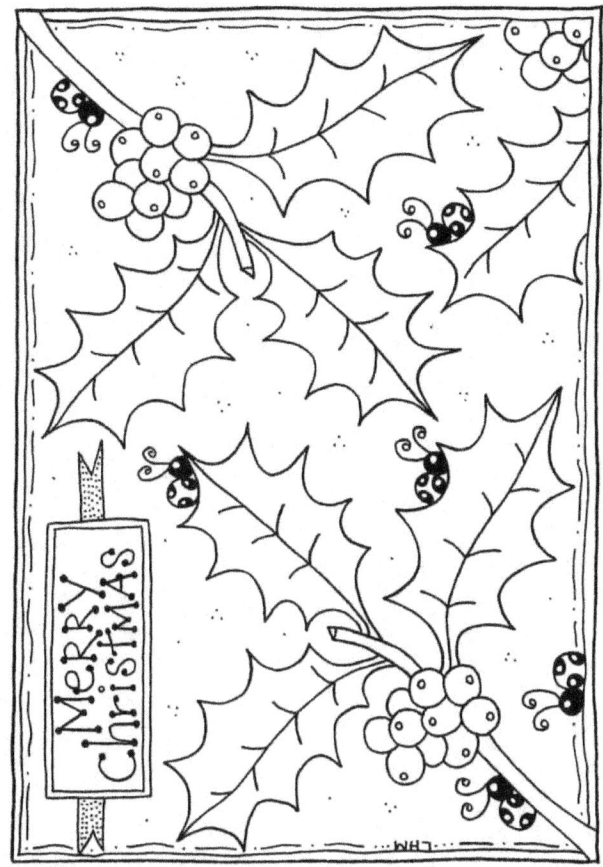
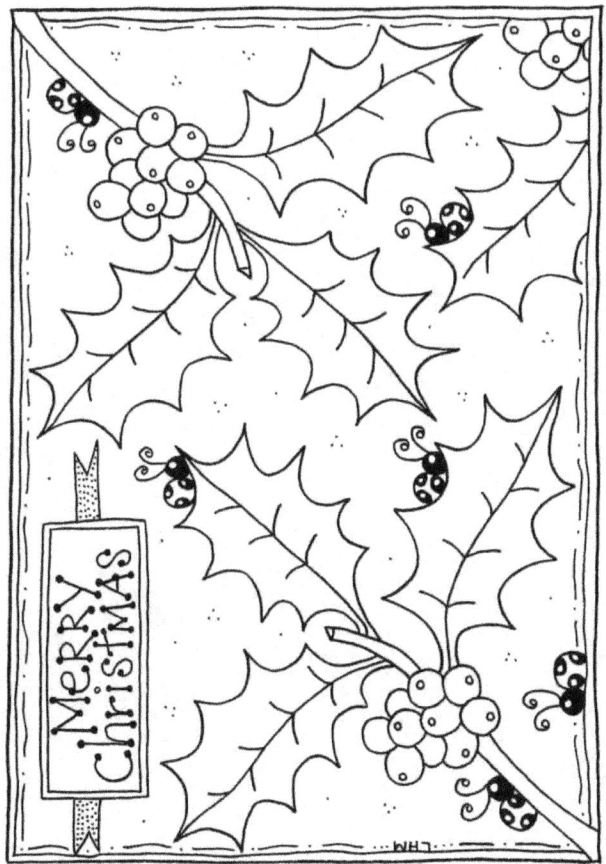
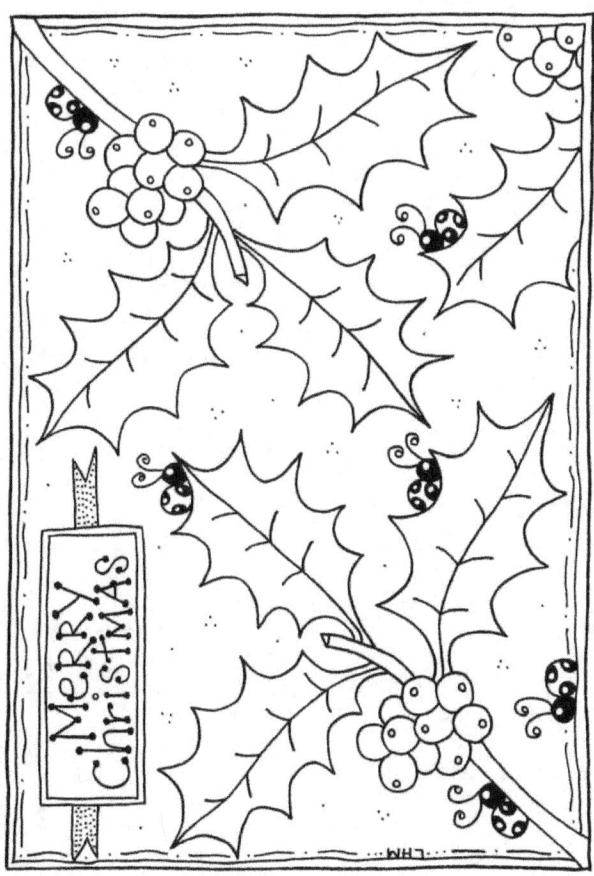

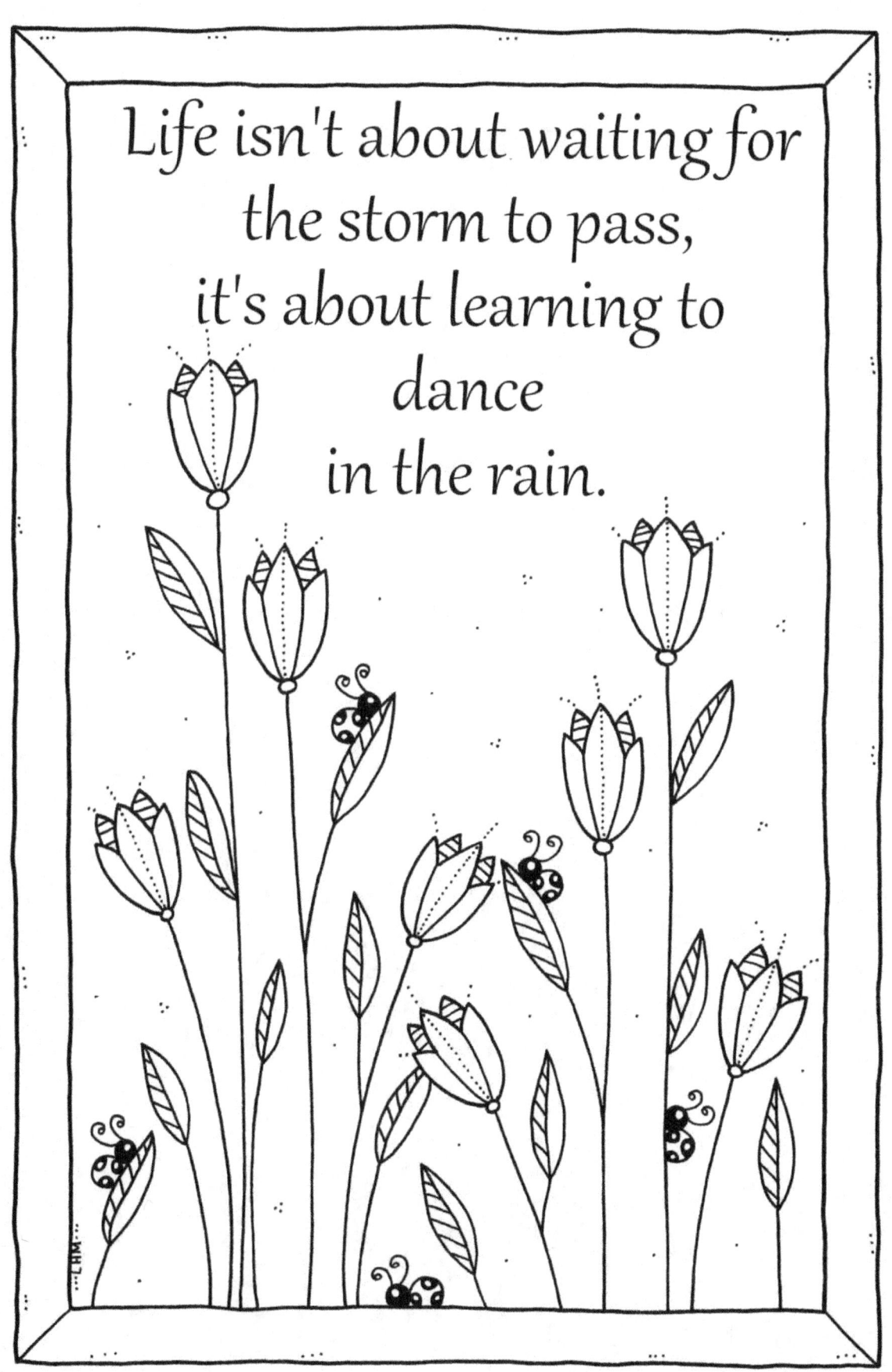

From my soon to be released Flower book.

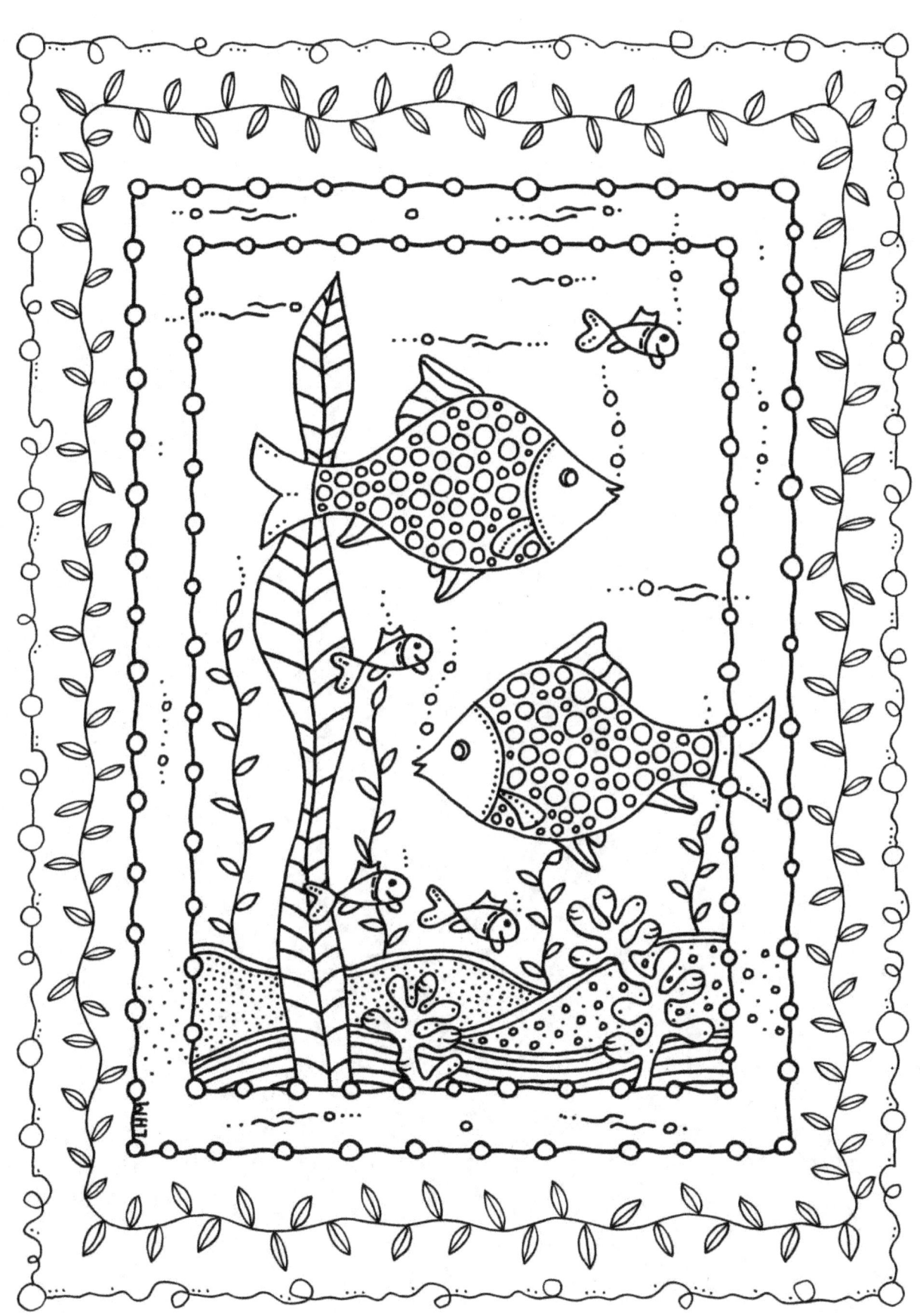

From my soon to be released Water book.

www.ingramcontent.com/pod-product-compliance
Lightning Source LLC
Chambersburg PA
CBHW062333220526

45469CB00008B/2695